MW00674542

Praise for Motivation at Work

"Laura has great insights regarding people's needs and what motivates them at work. She also delivers many practical suggestions for enhancing both job satisfaction and productivity. A valuable resource for anyone in business."
– **Hal Urban** Author of *Positive Words, Powerful Results*

"Wisdom, deep understanding, and inspiration for those who yearn to transform their organization into an environment that supports meaningful work. Laura Cardone, a wise woman, is a trusted guide that leads us on a step-by-step journey to 21st century business success."
– **Rev. Angela Peregoff**, Global Religious Science Minister

"Rarely have I seen a resource that speaks to your spirit and your bottom line. This is a must-read if you want to revolutionize your workplace and/or sustain profitability."
–**John Eggen**, President The Mission Marketing Mentors, Inc. www.missionmarketingmentors.com.

"I've had the opportunity to work with Laura firsthand and witness how her leadership approach can drive change and enthusiasm within an organization. I am delighted that her tools and strategies will be available as a resource to a broader spectrum of business owners and managers."
– **Kelly J. Hardy**, Vice President Client Services, Harris Connect, Inc.

"How can I motivate the people who work for me?" is one of the most common questions asked by business owners, managers, and supervisors. Laura Cardone's new book provides myriad answers -- practical, useful, and workable." – **BJ Gallagher**, coauthor of *YES Lives in the Land of NO: a Tale of Triumph over Negativity*

"If you want to inspire your employees and thrill your customers, this is one book you won't want to miss."
– **Susan L. Cunningham**, Certified Senior Advisor and Founder of Senior Resources Group Inc., Author of *Unwrapping the Sandwich Generation*

"The book is an enlightened read and provides clear step-by-step methods to create positive change. If you're looking to completely revamp your company, inspire your team or simply want to improve your personal leadership skills, this book will put you on the right path."
– **Marina Gray,** Sr. Merchandise Manager NetShops

"This is a must-read for any business owner or executive who wants to build a top performing business."
– **Aline Hanle**, Author and Owner *Beyond Fitness*

"Here is a helpful and easy-to-read resource that is profound in its scope and clarity. It's loaded with intelligent insights you can use to build a better workplace and a healthier bottom line!" – **Lina Penalosa**, President *The Write Solution*

"For enlightened leaders everywhere who know that work is an essential ingredient for a fulfilling life. Here are the tools and strategies to help you transform your business!"
– **Kristi Pederson**, CEO, Adventure In Art, INC.

"A results oriented approach that will help managers increase creativity and productivity in themselves and within their teams"
– **Irene Rivera de Royston**, Director Field Education Norfolk State University

"If you are a business owner or manager who wants to put the soul back into Corporate America, here's your opportunity. Take the challenge, make a difference and build a better business."
– **Cheryl Blossom**, Director The Institute for Inspired Living and Author of *Seven Days to a New You: Transform Your Life with Meditation and Visualization*

Motivation at Work

Transform Your Business in 6 Extraordinary Steps

Laura Cardone

Published By: Profits *with* Purpose, Inc.
2133-126 Upton DR #252 Virginia Beach, VA 23454

ISBN Print Edition: 978-0-9788334-0-4
ISBN Electronic Edition: 978-0-9788334-1-1

Library of Congress Cataloging-in-Publication Data

Cardone, Laura.
Motivation at work : transform your business in six extraordinary steps / Laura Cardone.
p. cm.
ISBN-13: 978-0-9788334-0-4
ISBN-10: 0-9788334-0-6

1. Employee motivation. 2. Personnel management.
3. Organizational change. 4. Success in business.
I. Title.

HF5549.5.M63C36 2006 658.3'14
QBI06-600322

CIP

It is our sincere hope that the Motivation-at-Work System will help you create the organization and business results you envision. This book is sold with the understanding that the author and publisher are not engaged in rendering personalized legal, accounting or professional services or advise. Readers are encouraged to seek the counsel of competent professionals with regard to such matters as interpretation of the law and business practices. The author and publisher shall not be liable or responsible to any person or entity with respect to any loss or damage caused, or alleged to have been caused, directly or indirectly, by the information contained in this book. If you do not wish to be bound by the terms stated above, please return this book for a full refund. This publication includes contact information for the author and additional resources. To the best of the author's and publisher's knowledge, the contact information is accurate as of the release date of this book.

Cover Design by Peri Poloni-Gabriel, Knockout Design, www.knockoutbooks.com
Interior Design and Editing by Bob Spear, Sharp Spear Enterprises

For permission requests, write to the publisher, addressed "Attention: Permissions Coordinator," at the address below.
Profits with Purpose Inc.
2133-126 Upton DR #252
Virginia Beach, VA 23454
Tel: (757) 426-3554
info@profitswithpurpose.com

For bulk purchases, call the office at (757) 426-3554
or email: sales@motivation-at-work.com

This book is dedicated to my family: my wise and wonderful husband Jim, my amazing daughter, Dawn and our awesome sons, Patrick and John. May you always dare to soar! You can be, do or create whatever you desire. May your hopes, dreams and goals be filled with the joyful promise of limitless discovery and great love!

To your ever-expanding potential!

Acknowledgments

It's hard to write something that adequately expresses thanks to all those who have helped me along my path. A book blends universal wisdom in addition to the author's unique thoughts, ideas, experiences, and relationships. My wish to you is that you celebrate and express fully your unique vision, in whatever way resonates with you. I hope you find my thoughts inspiring and helpful.

So in thanking all of those wonderful people who have come into my life, I wish to say up front that you are truly special to me. I certainly wish to leave no one out for you are all important, unique and limitless potential. I thank you whether your name is listed on these pages or not. With that said, know that you are appreciated and loved beyond what words can describe.

I wish to thank completely my family, and especially my husband Jim for his unflinching support. Without you, none of this would be possible. Dawn, Patrick and John you are truly amazing; thank you for being you. Mom, Dad, Karen and Jeff, thank you for being there and knowing when to laugh at those wonderfully quirky circumstances that are part of family.

For my good friends in our MMG, Lina, Sue, Angela and Lou, I say thank you, thank you and again thank you. You are awesome and your creative energy and insights are without parallel.

Thank you to John Eggen from Mission Publishing and Mission Marketing Mentors. Your mastery goes far beyond the publishing industry and for that I am truly grateful.

To Dolores, Don, Marina, Will, Kristi, Irene, Al, Carol, Sonny, Kathy and Howard, thank you for your wonderful friendship. Our relationships lift us up beyond where we can go as individuals. You are treasured friends, thank you for being you.

To my wonderful sisters, Michelle, Lou, Jan, Sara, Dianah, Laura, Sue and our guide, Angela at the Center for Mindful Studies, it is truly a pleasure. I am forever grateful that we met.

To Peri Poloni-Gabriel, my cover designer at Knockout Design. You have an amazing gift. Thank you for sharing your unique talents and intuition with me.

To Bob Spear, my editor and interior designer from Sharp Spear Enterprises. Thank you for your patience and attention to detail.

Contents

Chapter 1: Introduction

"Businesses are communities of people working toward a common purpose. To tap the tremendous unrealized potential that exists in all of us, we must think of work as an essential part of a fulfilling life. We can move past success to significance when we realize our purpose is found in serving others, and connecting to something that goes far beyond the bottom line."

~Laura Cardone

The Journey Ahead

You are beginning a journey of transformation that will take your business to the next level. The six-step *Motivation-at-Work* System will help you eliminate the frustration of unrealized potential. As we move through each step, you will learn how to resolve the specific issues that are depleting the positive energy in your workplace.

As you implement the proven strategies, resources and tools, you will be creating a unique vision of a *Perfect Workplace*. When you do this, you create a *Top Performing Business*. You will be part of an elite group of businesses that consistently achieve top financial performance. But, more importantly, you will connect with something that goes far beyond the bottom line. You'll be creating a business community filled with energetic, enthusiastic

and respectful employees that work toward a common goal, past success to significance.
Motivation is a powerful word. It literally means to *inspire, energize, galvanize, inspirit, move, or propel.* On the other hand, to demotivate means to depress, devalue, impair, sadden, and push down.

Imagine you have to choose to work on one of two teams. The first team feels depressed and devalued; they are de-motivated. The second team feels inspired and energized; they are motivated. Which team is capable of high achievement? Which team would you want to join? Undoubtedly you would choose the Top Performing Team—the inspired organization.
The good news; people don't start out unmotivated. In fact, people overwhelmingly are very excited when they start a new job. They become disengaged over time. This means there is a cause and effect relationship. It means people who are "de-motivated" can change. We'll cover the reasons why people disengage, and the specific strategies you can use to transform your business into an inspired, high achievement culture.

The Benefits

The benefits of a highly engaged, *Top Performing Workforce* are beyond powerful.

A *Top Performing Team*:

1) Provides you with an incredible competitive advantage

2) Significantly improves employee retention

3) Increases overall productivity

4) Cultivates superior quality products and services

5) Propels your customer satisfaction to new heights

6) Broadens your opportunities to expand your business

7) Saves you money as you identify and improve ineffective or inefficient practices
8) Increases customer retention and the lifetime value of your customers
9) Reduces the likelihood of stress or work related illness

10) Boosts your bottom line to top tier status

11) Enables long-term growth and viability

12) Improves attendance because people actually want to come to work

13) Creates an atmosphere of accomplishment, excitement and fun where people want to actively participate

14) Helps you build a pool of internal talent who want to grow with your company

15) Creates a happier and healthier environment

16) Helps you attract the top talent in your industry

17) Improves your community image and improves the quality of the work lives that you touch

18) Reduces the amount of time you spend putting out fires

19) Generates innovative thinking and new opportunities

20) Enables you to focus on business development, strategic planning, or whatever else you can't get to today

You Choose

You can choose to continue down your current path, or not. You can choose to dismiss the six-step *Motivation-at-Work strategies,* or not. It is entirely up to you. As you read this, you may find that something resonates with you. That it just makes sense. I sincerely hope this book helps you transform your organization into a

community of inspired people who are enthusiastic about their work, who feel they too are a part of something extraordinary. I hope it inspires you to challenge the limiting beliefs that prevent you and your team from reaching your tremendous potential.
I do appreciate the challenges business owners face. This isn't just theory or empty research speaking. I come from practical experience, and a deep knowing that there's so much more that we can do to create meaningful and fulfilling work. When we do that, we also create a better business, and a richer work life for the people who choose to put their trust in us as leaders.

We are at an interesting point in business history. Business owners, executives, employees, and customers are no longer content with business as usual.

Customers are fed up with lackluster service. A study released in March 2006 by Harris Interactive® reported that *96%* of U.S. adults said they've had bad customer service experiences in the past year. [1] Of those surveyed, 80% said they'd stopped doing business with a company because of a poor customer service experience. To top it off, once they do stop doing business with you, virtually no one (0%) indicated they'd come back without some type of incentive to win them back.

Employees feel disconnected, undervalued and unappreciated. People are job hopping in record numbers. A paycheck is simply not enough. They are searching for meaningful work.

Leaders, on the other hand, are frustrated by less than stellar employee enthusiasm, loyalty and commitment. Employee retention and recruitment challenges continue to plague many business owners.

During my 25+ year career, I've been a business owner, a Director for a Fortune 50 company, a Vice President for a family owned company, an author, and worked with thousands of business managers and employees on countless business improvement programs and initiatives. There is a common pattern of limiting beliefs and behaviors that keep organizations from creating a high achievement culture.

You can uncover those limiting beliefs and discover your true potential in the steps ahead.

The vast majority of employees I have met want to be part of something special. They want to contribute in a meaningful way and help their business team do well. In this book, we're going to review what you can do to tap that commitment, loyalty and enthusiasm that's just waiting to be brought into your workplace.

People drive business results. Today's workers are not satisfied with jobs that provide only a paycheck. Everyone wants fulfilling work! We all want to feel good about what we do. We want to make a difference, and a "valued" contribution. Your team is no different.

When you reconnect with your team and give them a reason to be inspired, amazing things happen. Your workplace becomes a place filled with energetic and committed people who are proud of the work they do. Your profits grow as your workplace gets stronger. Everyone wants to be on a winning team. You can lead champions if you're willing to challenge the thinking and behaviors that limit potential.

Albert Einstein once said you can't solve a problem with the same thinking that created it in the first place. Businesses cannot continue to put their organization's cultural health on the back burner and expect it to carry them and their company to big profits. It just doesn't work that way. If you want different results, you simply have to change your thinking.

How This Works

This program is designed to be followed in a logical progression. Each step builds on the prior step. But, you won't have to wait until you've completed all six steps to start seeing improvements in your workplace. The *Motivation-at-Work* system was designed to help you create positive energy and commitment with the very first steps.

This book does provide you with a complete six-step system, but it is also designed to be a reference guide you can continue to use for years to come. Use the headlines in each chapter to help you find the information you're looking for.

In some steps, you are given exercises to complete. Wherever possible, engage your team to help you with these exercises. When you do this, breakthrough ideas emerge, and you build enthusiasm and trust.

There are many templates included in this book to help you move through each step faster. There's also a planning chapter and exercises to help you reduce potential obstacles. The strategies presented in Step 4 help you remove the barriers that are blocking your team's potential.

Don't forget to check out www.motivation-at-work.com for additional strategies, templates and resources. Log in on the client access page. As a book purchaser you can access the client area by entering the username team and password spirit.

So, let's get started!

Chapter 2: An Overview

Employee Motivation: How We Arrived Here & The Journey Ahead

"If your people are headed in the wrong direction,
don't motivate them."

~George Odiorne

Consider your team—

Do they arrive at your workplace energized to do their best work?

How much effort do they enthusiastically commit to help your organization succeed?

If they are unhappy with their jobs, do you think they will be highly motivated to help you build long term customer relationships, improve processes, lower operating costs, eagerly contribute innovative solutions, or actively contribute to your business growth? Probably not.

Job satisfaction, employee motivation and the health of your business are tightly intertwined. When spirit is low, energy flows slowly and in the opposite direction of your goals. Your organization's potential is unrealized and your spiritual and financial bottom lines suffer.

Let's look at the impact. According to the 2005 U.S. Job Recovery and Retention Survey released in November 2005, a full 76% of employees surveyed were looking for new employment opportunities because they were not satisfied in their current workplace. This is unthinkable when you consider the impact job satisfaction has on our health, happiness, and our businesses.

If you believe, as I do, that work is an essential ingredient for a fulfilling life, then it's time to get serious about doing everything we can to create positive and fulfilling work experiences. This truly will feed your soul and your bottom line. It will forever change the way we do business.

Imagine what would happen . . . if we thought of work as an essential ingredient of a fulfilling life?

Imagine what would happen . . . if we knew that we could create anything we wanted?

Imagine what would happen ... if we knew we could not fail?

You can do, be, or create anything you desire and enjoy the journey!

In this chapter, you will discover the critical contributors to motivation and what you can do to lift up your workplace spirit and your bottom line. You'll also learn why many organizations struggle to achieve their goals and objectives, and what practices and processes need to be aligned to create an organization filled with people who:

- ☐ Are enthusiastic about their work
- ☐ Are highly engaged and productive
- ☐ Genuinely want to help you and your company succeed

We'll also review the fundamental drivers for employee motivation and why people become unmotivated in the first place. You'll get an overview of the six-step process that will help you transform your organization into the business you want, and you'll understand the practices and processes that have the most impact on the health of your organization.

Motivation 101—The Fundamentals

So, how do you motivate people? By reconnecting with the human spirit that inspires success, and never forgetting that the individuals on your team drive everything. The beliefs and attitudes of your workforce determine the outcomes of your processes, the quality of your products, your customer and vendor relationships, and *your bottom line.* The connection between the human spirit and operating a business is the critical element that is missing in many organizations. It is why employee satisfaction and motivation are at low points in many organizations across North America.

How do you reconnect with the spirit? By getting to the root of what drives human behavior and letting that guide your actions in business. At the very core of human nature, we are programmed to avoid pain or move away from what is unpleasant. We move toward what makes us feel good. You and I will actively seek out opportunities that make us feel good about what we do at work, and we will avoid situations that make us feel bad.

Who controls this? Leaders. The leaders in any organization, from the front line supervisors to the senior executives are the individuals with the most influence over whether individuals feel good or bad about their work.

There are seven common reasons why people leave an organization. No matter how you dress it up or what you call it, the reasons for changing jobs almost always fall into one of these seven categories.[2]

The 7 Reasons Why People Leave

1. The job or the workplace is not as expected.
2. Poor job fit
3. Insufficient coaching or feedback
4. Not enough opportunities for growth and development

5. Feeling undervalued and unrecognized
6. Stress from work life balance issues
7. Loss of trust in senior leadership

You're probably surprised because "more money" or "better benefits" didn't make the list. Those are the standard answers provided by departing employees on exit interviews. However, after analyzing the data from close to 20,000 interviews, the Saratoga Institute found money is rarely the real reason why people leave. The plain truth is the majority of people who leave will not disclose the *real reasons* why they are leaving. The "more money" reason is an easy excuse for exiting employees. Most workers will not risk burning bridges, so they do not disclose the real reasons why they leave or what motivated them to start looking in the first place.

I have worked with companies in some of the *lowest paying industries*, but they had higher productivity, lower turnover, happier employees, and a healthier workplace *and bottom line* than their competitors who were paying much higher wages.

How did these organizations compete for and retain top talent in such a competitive environment?

1. They connected with their workforce on a personal level.
2. They developed highly effective managers who understood the connection between their behavior and the health of their organization's culture and financial performance.
3. They used consistent practices that helped them get the right people in the right positions.
4. They continuously provided opportunities for their team members to grow and learn.

When you examine these four factors—it becomes apparent who has the most influence over job satisfaction in any organization. It is your leaders and primarily your managers who impact your outcomes.

Manager behaviors created the environment you are working in today! Ultimately it is the management team in any company that drives employee satisfaction levels, and therefore morale and motivation.

The Leader as Architect

The best business leaders create highly motivated workplaces by acting as architects. They purposefully design, plan, coordinate, and guide their organizations. Think of this role as a *Chief Workplace Architect* that provides the vision, the tools and strategies to create a healthy and robust workplace. Depending on the size and structure of your organization, this may be a business owner, executive, or human resources director.

The *Motivation-at-Work* system lays out this process in six steps and provides you with the tools and strategies to transform your organization into the business you envision. The system helps you:

1. Accurately assess the issues that are limiting your organization's performance

2. Plan effectively so you can achieve your desired results faster and with less effort

3. Create a compelling vision and effective goals that move you and your organization toward your desired outcomes

4. Choose the most effective strategies to address your unique requirements and goals

5. Inspire and develop your managers to raise your financial and cultural performance to the next level

6. Continue to reap the rewards of a *Perfect Workplace* and *Top Performing Business* committed to ongoing growth and improvement

When you engage your team in the visioning and planning processes and actively manage your cultural health, you create the foundation for high achievement and meaningful work. Highly motivated environments don't just happen—they are created! That's exactly what the *Motivation-at-Work* system was designed to do; provide you with an easy to follow blueprint that will help you build the business you envision.

Would you develop a new product or service without careful research and planning? Of course not; you would develop a blue print and a prototype before you started to mass produce a new product or service.

You can achieve significant improvements whether you own the company, or manage a division or department. Of course if you want to achieve *companywide* improvements, transformation efforts should to be driven from the senior executive level in your organization.

Why People Become Unmotivated

There are many reasons why motivation declines. There are also common circumstances such as rapid growth, job or organizational restructuring, and management changes that can de-motivate your work team. Regardless of the circumstances, there are perceptions or beliefs that are commonly shared by employees who disengage and become unmotivated.

These employees:

1. Don't feel recognized or appreciated

2. Don't think their manager or employer values them or their input

3. Don't trust their employer

4. Feel disconnected and lack a sense of community

5. Don't understand how their contributions impact other departments, the bottom line or their customers

6. Perceive inconsistencies in the way policies are applied and job performance is rated

7. May be in a poor fitting job. They accepted a promotion or new job for the wrong reasons (usually for a pay increase, but their job doesn't use their natural strengths).

8. Lack clarity about their job performance. They may not understand the expectations of their supervisor, or perhaps the expectations are inconsistent.

How We Got Here

Why is it such a struggle to create an enthusiastic and committed work team? What can we do to create an environment that supports fulfilling work and a high performance business?

Although each organization has unique characteristics, there are common problems and dysfunctional practices that tend to surface in many organizations. These practices are like bad habits that redirect your focus away from your positive intentions. A dysfunctional workplace practice robs you of the meaningful human relationships that propel you to top performer status and a joyful business.

The goods news; habits can be changed. Your past does not predict your future, unless you let it. The fact that you're reading this means you're committed to creating an extraordinary workplace. You'll find it's within your reach when you follow the six-step system.

Many companies have walked the same path you have and created amazing transformations. Companies that create committed, enthusiastic teams, consistently perform in the top 20% in their respective industries. But, financial gain is only one of the many rewards you receive when you create top performing teams. Your organization has unlimited potential! As you learn, grow and expand that potential, you will be creating something that moves past success to significance. You will be creating a community of people blessed with meaningful work!

Five Unhealthy Practices to Avoid

1. **Excessive short term, task orientation.** Western culture encourages the frantic activity that can easily make us believe that we are human doings instead of human beings. So, it's not a giant leap when leaders get caught up in short range thinking. We have been conditioned to continuously check

the next thing off our never ending to-do lists. This type of thinking creates a disconnected workplace. It does not build the skills that will take your business to the next level. In this type of environment, there's little attention given to creating a dynamic work community that supports long term growth.

2. **Misdirected planning**. Many organizations fail to create sufficient plans or strategies in the one area that will give them the most leverage. Detailed plans are almost always created when developing products, changing processes, budgeting and forecasting sales. But, organizations often fail to create a plan for the highest impact area; workplace culture. Communication is done haphazardly at best, and few formal programs or practices exist to build the high quality environment that is needed to produce a top performing company.

3. **Not training, coaching, and developing managers, supervisors, and executives.** Would you prepare a team for the Olympics without a coach or the appropriate training tools? Unfortunately that is what happens in many business organizations. Leadership development tends to fall at the bottom of business priorities, and over time, it takes a major toll on a company's performance. So, the next time you're tempted to cut a development program in order to reduce expenses, remember the wise words of Albert Einstein. "We can't solve problems by using the same kind of thinking we used when we created them." You will continue to get the same thinking and practices time and time again, unless you do something to break the cycle. Training and development is a way to introduce new ways of thinking that can take your business to the next level.

4. **Unexpected economic factors or demand that leads to rapid growth or downsizing.** This gets everyone into survival mode and often companies never step out of this vicious cycle. Executives and manager don't *make the time* to create or rebuild the foundation; one that will get them where they want to go over the long haul.

5. **Poor hiring practices.** Many companies assume managers and supervisors know how to select the best job candidates. Not

> true, most people make their hiring decisions within the first 2 to 4 minutes of the interview. So most hiring managers never get past the surface to confirm job fit, let alone verify that a candidate can really deliver what they advertised in that well-packaged resume.

Consider the current activities in your company. Overall, where do the managers, supervisors, and employees primarily focus? On tasks? Processes? Financial Statements? Sales? Customer Service? Marketing efforts? Fostering employee relationships? Training? Planning?

Most companies spend the majority of their time reacting to task requests. So, people naturally feel disconnected, undervalued, and unmotivated.

Transform Your Workplace in Six Steps

In the six step *Motivation-at-Work* system you'll learn how to build your vision of a *Perfect Workplace*, so you can create a *Top Performing Business*. Each chapter gives you strategies, tips, tools, and simple, cost-effective ideas to help you minimize potential obstacles.

To be effective over the long term, an employee motivation program will need to:

Help you connect with your workforce on a personal level. Your employees want to feel their contributions make a difference. They want to feel appreciated. No one wants to be a number. We are social creatures and need to feel like our work has meaning beyond earning a paycheck.

Develop highly effective, enlightened managers. This means managers motivate their teams by using strategies that build up their workplace. They don't tear it apart by using fear and intimidation to motivate. Enlightened managers take responsibility for their ongoing development and growth. However, you need to provide support and encouragement to build a highly motivated workplace.

Use practices that ensure good job fit. This means hiring and succession practices that take into account aptitude and work history, as well as behavioral traits that fit the position, and the environment you want to create. The work landscape is littered with bad boss stories and bad hiring decisions. I am amazed by the number of companies that take it for granted that their managers know how to interview, hire and promote effectively. This is simply not the case. The majority of hiring and placement decisions are based on subjective measures. Most placement decisions have little to do with whether a candidate can and will do the job well. Consistent processes are needed to ensure good results for your business and the people you choose to hire and promote.

Continuously provide opportunities for your team members to grow and learn. A study conducted by the ASTD (American Society for Training and Development) of 575 publicly traded U.S. firms confirmed that companies that were in the top quarter of per-employee training investments produced *24% higher net profits and 218% higher income per employee.* The study analyzed the training investments and financial results of 575 publicly traded U.S. firms. [3]

Don't panic; the cost of training and development does not have to break the bank. There are a lot of cost effective strategies that you can tailor to your organization's budget. We'll be covering these strategies in detail in steps four and five.

Practices and Processes that Impact Employee Motivation

The strategies and ideas you will discover in the upcoming chapters were chosen to help you refine the practices and processes that directly impact employee motivation. You'll find many cost effectives strategies to help you shine in these critical areas. The areas listed here determine the overall health of your organization.

- ☐ Manager and leadership behaviors
- ☐ Recognizing and rewarding top performance
- ☐ Quality focus

- ☐ Customer service orientation
- ☐ Commitment, enthusiasm, and respect
- ☐ Opportunities to participate in decision making and empowering team members
- ☐ Long-term orientation
- ☐ Employee satisfaction and morale
- ☐ Hiring and Succession Practices
- ☐ Performance Management
- ☐ Fair compensation

But before you start making changes to your current business practices, you will need to determine exactly where you are today, and where you want to go. By doing this, you'll be able to choose the most effective strategies for your organization. You'll also learn how to minimize potential obstacles as you create your high achievement culture.

The system was designed to help you get results as you move through each step. So, you won't have to wait until you've completed every step before you see improvements in your workplace. You'll find out more when you read each chapter. But for now, here's a summary of the six step process.

To easily remember the six steps, think S.P.I.R.I.T. A system that helps you energize, inspire, and create the team that you envision.

The Six-Step Recap—Think S.P.I.R.I.T

Survey ⇨ Plan ⇨ Imagine ⇨ Reflect & Design ⇨ Inspire ⇨ Transform

Step 1: SURVEY
In this step, you assess your current situation and create a benchmark so you can measure your progress. It's important to invest time up front validating any assumptions you might have about root causes of underperformance. Just as you would invest time to research a new market, you will want to determine the underlying beliefs and attitudes that are responsible for your workplace and results today. This helps you choose the strategies that will give you the best results. Templates, detailed instructions,

and suggested tools are included in this chapter. You'll probably discover that this step takes far less time than you might think.

Step 2: PLAN
In this step, you are setting the stage for maximum impact. Like any big change, you will want to set yourself up for success with a good plan and get the right people involved at the right time. If you don't take the time to plan now, you'll lose momentum later due to unnecessary delays. Please resist the urge to jump ahead. A little extra time spent planning will get you where you want to be much faster and with less resistance.

Step 3: IMAGINE
In this step, you will define your *perfect* or your *ideal* workplace. This is where you get absolute clarity around your vision, and where you create very specific goals. In this step, you actively engage your team to help you create a workplace filled with people who are enthusiastic and committed to the success of your organization. By engaging your team in the process, you'll start building positive energy and a better business.

Once you've assessed your current situation, set the stage for success with a solid plan, and defined your vision and goals, it's time to move to the next step.

Step 4: REFLECT & DESIGN
In this step, you pull all of the pieces together to address the gaps between where you are today (*your current situation*) and where you want to go (*your Perfect Workplace*).
When you d*esign*, you choose the strategies that close those gaps so you can create the *Top Performing Business* and *Perfect Workplace* you envision. You'll use the strategies in this chapter to select specific actions that address the gaps in your organization. Those actions become a part of your plan.

Step 5: INSPIRE YOUR MANAGERS
In this step, you inspire and develop a simple plan to develop the leadership skills that will help you create lasting change. Your management team will drive your success, so they will need to know and practice the management behaviors that create a top performing culture. The benefits of inspired and effective

managers cannot be overstated. Leadership behaviors that support a high performing workplace are absolutely critical to the success of any employee motivation program. You can get small lifts in productivity by changing compensation and introducing incentive programs, but without the right management practices, you'll quickly revert back to prior performance levels.

Step 6: TRANSFORM
In this step, you make your changes stick and keep your momentum going. Like quality improvement programs, workplace regeneration programs require ongoing evaluation and refinement. Business conditions and circumstances change, so strategies and practices can get stale and lose their effectiveness over time. This step helps you continue to create *Top Performing Business* benefits for years to come.

As you proceed through these steps, you'll find hundreds of low or no cost tips, tools, and strategies to help you create positive results.

Connect with your vision and goals regularly as you move through the six step transformation process. Imagine what would happen if everyone in your organization was committed to creating a *Perfect Workplace* and *Top Performing Business.* Connecting with the end result will help you create consistent and compelling messages that get everyone moving in the desired direction.

Leader Beliefs—The Power to Move Mountains

Over the years, I've met a few skeptical executives and business owners who felt people should just be content to have a paycheck. My questions to these leaders were—would you be energized by a boss with that attitude? How motivated would you be to help him or her succeed? Leader beliefs directly influence the health of their workplace.

The attitudes we bring to work are formed by our past experiences. We adopt them, usually unconsciously, from our family, schoolmates, friends and workplace mentors and peers.

To create a better workplace, examine and challenge the shared workplace beliefs in your organization.

Consider the beliefs and attitudes below and note which ones you've used, witnessed, or heard expressed by managers in your organization. Some may seem outrageous, but I have worked with many clients who had unknowingly adopted these limiting beliefs. Although thoughts are not always directly expressed, actions don't lie. It's only when we shed light on limiting beliefs and behaviors that we can deal effectively with them. Once you become aware of them, you can diffuse the power they have to limit your results.

Unenlightened Leader Beliefs

- □ Who said life was going to be fair anyway?
- □ Work isn't supposed to be fun. That's why they call it work.
- □ Go for the paycheck. You'll get used to the new *job/boss/70 hour work week*.
- □ Make him a manger; he's the top producer.
- □ There's little to gain with ongoing training and development. It's an unnecessary expense, besides we don't have the time.
- □ Do as I say, not as I do.
- □ Pull yourself up by your bootstraps and deal with it.
- □ I've paid my dues, I'm an executive now. I don't have to…*talk to front line employees, deal with unhappy customers, walk the floor, work nights or weekends, or get my hands dirty.*
- □ It's not my problem you can't find a good baby sitter. I don't care if you don't have someone you trust to take care of your child.
- □ What do you mean you're leaving to have dinner with your family? You've only worked ten hours today. This report is far more important to me than your family!
- □ Employees are just out to milk me for everything they can.

Consider carefully the actions and attitudes that evolve over time because even though they may not be verbalized, your employees and customers can *hear* them clearly.
Now imagine the difference in how employees and customers would react to the *Enlightened Leader* beliefs.

Enlightened Leader Beliefs

- ☐ Let's figure out together how we can reach our goals!
- ☐ Why not have fun while we're doing it?
- ☐ Is this position a good fit for your interests? Does it use your inherent strengths?
- ☐ Make her a manager: she's a great coach; she listens well; is highly respected; and knows how to build teams that get results.
- ☐ I practice what I preach.
- ☐ Get input from the frontline; they understand the issues and know how to fix them.
- ☐ I need help developing my communication skills. How do you recommend I…?
- ☐ Let's put our heads together and come up with a solution that addresses your concerns and mine.
- ☐ I am grateful for the contributions and sacrifices our employees make every day. I provide the tools and support they need to be successful. I stay connected with my customers and employees so I know how to create a company that is successful over the long-term.
- ☐ The problem of finding quality and affordable daycare is becoming a big problem for a number of employees. Let's get together with some local daycare providers and employees to brainstorm solutions. How can we expect our working parents to be highly motivated when they are understandably concerned about the welfare of their children?
- ☐ When was the last time you *…took a vacation? Had dinner with your family?* I appreciate your dedication and willingness to put in long hours, but don't neglect your personal life. People who balance their personal and professional lives are more productive, and are less likely to experience job burnout. You're a valued member of this team, please take care of yourself!
- ☐ My employees are truly the greatest asset in my organization. They are why we are so successful!

Who would you want to work for—the *unenlightened leader* or the *enlightened leader*? Where would you want to invest your valuable time? Which leader would inspire you to go the extra mile? Which workplace would you be proud to call your employer?

Moving Forward

A company with a highly motivated workforce will be far more profitable, and will retain their customers and employees much longer than a business that has an unhealthy work environment. *Top Performing Companies* contribute more than just jobs to their local economy. They make a positive difference in the lives of the people they touch: their customers, employees, vendors, and the local community organizations they support.

Employees who are loyal and motivated to do their very best have a compelling reason for being that way. Such loyalty and high performance is earned and doesn't just happen over night.

You can start creating a high energy, highly motivated organization immediately. The return to your bottom line is significant and real. In fact, most of the organizations that have applied the principles you will learn in this system, achieved double digit net profit improvements.

But, there are also improvements that you can't measure on a financial statement. These changes impact you in a personal and very meaningful way. These immeasurable changes also enrich the quality of your team's workplace experience. The transformation to a *Perfect Workplace* helps you create joy in work, and a better life for your employees and customers.

You can make a very real difference starting now! Serve as a role model and challenge everyone in your company to start examining their limiting beliefs and behaviors. Partner with your employees, managers, suppliers and customers to create truly amazing results! Take care of your employees and they will take care of you.

Now let's get started with step one!

Chapter 3 | Step 1: Survey

"Each problem has a hidden opportunity so powerful that it literally dwarfs the problem. The greatest success stories were created by people who recognized a problem and turned it into an opportunity."

~ Joseph Sugarman

Are you frustrated by productivity issues, low morale, or are you just tired of business as usual? In this chapter, you will uncover the limiting beliefs that are hindering your organization's performance. Once you understand the obstacles, you can effectively remove them. This clears the way for you to create a better workplace AND achieve your financial and operating objectives.

You cannot achieve consistent, top business results without having a highly motivated team…and you won't have a highly motivated team without having a great workplace.

What's a great workplace? It's a business filled with high-energy people who are committed to their individual success as well as the success of their teammates, and the success of the company in which they work.

You can tell when you walk into a great workplace by observing the:

- ☐ Superior quality of their work
- ☐ Smiles and positive energy
- ☐ Enthusiastic and friendly interaction with customers

- □ Highly engaged managers and staff
- □ Outstanding financial performance

But, before you can design a program that will help you create an great workplace, you will need to understand *exactly* where you are today. This is known as the assessment stage or analyzing your current situation.

WARNING: Please do not skip this step. Its human nature to believe we know what is broken when we are in the environment day in and day out. However, this is the very reason you should resist making assumptions. Sometimes we are too close and may draw conclusions too quickly. So, we can miss critical information that can help us accurately diagnose a problem. Assuming a root cause without validation is like trying to read the *outside* label when you are standing *inside* the jar. We simply can't see the big picture when our view point is limited.

To create the workplace and business results you want, you will need a realistic understanding of your current situation. The insights you will gain by completing this step will also help you choose the best solutions, and prioritize your strategies so you can achieve your desired benefits faster.

In this chapter, you'll discover a fast, affordable and effective way to develop and deploy a survey that will uncover the beliefs that are driving your current results. This process also gives you a means of measuring progress as you implement the strategies that will take your business to the next level. You will also learn:

- □ How to diagnose the causes behind the symptoms

- □ The three keys for getting an accurate diagnosis

- □ The power of asking the right questions

- □ How to ask questions that enable solutions

- □ The advantages of web survey tools

- □ The six steps for creating powerful surveys

- ☐ Survey best practices
- ☐ The personal and professional value of a healthier workplace
- ☐ Sample employee satisfaction survey questions
- ☐ Guidelines for designing your own survey
- ☐ How to identify and interview your informal leaders
- ☐ The importance of setting the stage when communicating your survey results

Treat the Causes Not the Symptoms

Just as a doctor diagnoses an illness and finds the cure by reviewing the symptoms first, you too will create your treatment plan by using a similar process. Like a doctor, you will review both qualitative and quantitative information and, *above all else*, you will ask questions to confirm your theories, feelings, and assumptions. It is a simple process, and does not require a lot of time, but it is a critical first step. Like a good doctor, always verify what you believe to be broken by asking the right questions.

Symptoms are things that are tangible, that you can observe and measure such as:

- ☐ Employee absenteeism
- ☐ Employee turnover
- ☐ Customer satisfaction
- ☐ Production output
- ☐ Market share data
- ☐ Sales trends

The trends tell you whether the symptom is getting better or getting worse. As these metrics increase or decrease, you can determine whether your organization is getting healthier, growing, in need of a tune up, or has one foot in the grave.

You can use the methods described here to gain insights about your current culture, the perceptions of your team members, and the causes that keep you and your business team from achieving the results you want.

The Three Keys to Getting an Accurate Diagnosis:

1. Use anonymous employee surveys to get candid feedback.

2. Review your performance trends.

3. Talk to your informal leaders.

We'll cover these three important methods in this chapter. But, before moving on, it's important to review how you will get the best possible information to help you uncover the root causes behind the symptoms.

The Power of Asking the Right Questions

Your team's thinking about your business and how it affects them personally and professionally created your current reality.

The perceptions, beliefs, and attitudes of your staff, managers, and executives drive your business results and what your customers think about your business. Your *team,* for purposes of creating a better business, must include input from *all levels* and in *all areas* of your organization.

Beliefs about how things are working (or *not working*) can vary by job function and across departments and divisions. These differences can provide valuable insights about the scope of the issues that are limiting your team's performance. This information can also help you identify leadership talent and practices you can tap to help you build a business with unlimited potential.

There is great power in asking the right questions for two reasons:

1. The right questions help you uncover the beliefs and perceptions that created your current performance results. The answers will tell you exactly what you need to fix or fine tune to get the results you want.

AND

2. A good question can create a shift in thinking. This leads to smarter strategies that move your organization forward faster.

The questions we ask lead to conclusions and perceptions that drive our actions and the corresponding results. It looks like this:

Questions⇨ Thoughts⇨ Actions⇨ Our Results

So how do you ask good survey questions?

- ☐ Ask yourself first, what is it you want and need to learn?
- ☐ KISS—**K**eep **I**t **S**hort and **S**imple.
- ☐ Break down complex questions if needed into multiple shorter questions.
- ☐ Plan for "Don't Know" or "Not Applicable" responses unless you are certain every respondent will have a clear answer.
- ☐ Remove obstacles by providing tools that promote candid, constructive answers and feedback.
- ☐ Provide tools that allow everyone in your organization to give you feedback. Consider developing vendor, partner and customer satisfaction surveys as well. You will benefit immensely from their perspectives!
- ☐ Choose your words carefully to get the best answer. For example, let's assume that your customer satisfaction ratings are dropping drastically. Customer complaints are up, and your business is losing market share at an alarming rate. To accurately assess employee attitudes about customer service

compared to everything else in their job description—would you ask: "*Is customer satisfaction important in our company?*" Or, "*Do you believe that customer satisfaction is a top priority at our company?*" Subtle difference, but by using *top priority* versus the generic *important*, you'll get a better read because *important* is much more subjective. On the other hand—TOP PRORITY is pretty darn clear.

- □ Don't shoot the messenger when the information isn't what you expected. This may seem obvious. However, I have been surprised by the very intelligent, caring executives who instantly shut down the flow of critical information because they react harshly when presented with "bad news." Trust and open exchange are the life blood of every top performing organization that consistently outperforms their competition year after year. So coach your managers about the importance of honest feedback and how it is absolutely necessary for resolving issues and achieving top performance.

If companies invested the same amount of energy planning their cultural objectives as they do their financial and productivity goals, they wouldn't need to waste time and money trying to make a round peg fit into a square hole.

Culture and financial performance are so closely interconnected that you cannot change one without impacting the other. The key to top performance is creating cultural goals that support your financial objectives so they work together instead of against each other.

Employee Surveys: Questions that Enable Solutions

To create a better workplace and significantly improve your financial performance—ask the right questions. Employee surveys are the tried and true way to get the information you need to get a solid view of your team's beliefs. Again, this understanding is critical because beliefs drive your performance.

The best way to uncover what's driving your results is to find out what your team thinks about the things that influence your productivity, quality, customer relationships, morale, leaders, culture, and your bottom line. There are a number of ways you can survey your team, including:

- Hiring a consultant or service to do it for you. This can be cost-prohibitive and time consuming. This method can cost you hundreds of thousands of dollars and take weeks to complete. Ouch!

- Do it yourself using the pen and pencil method. This option does not promote candor as information is typically not received anonymously. It will also take a lot of effort to compile and analyze the information.

- Internal email surveys or the "hit reply" method. Okay this one is fast to set up, but you will not get the candid feedback you need to build a better business. If you can identify the source of the response you will significantly reduce participation and candor.

- Use web tools and services to survey your team. This method promotes the candor you need to get good answers. It is easy to set up and inexpensive to do and most online survey systems provide reporting tools that make it very easy to get the information you need quickly.

I focus on web tools and services here because it is an affordable and effective way for you to get good, candid information. It's an approach that can help you implement your workplace improvements faster.

What if you have some team members who do not have internet access?

There are a number of things you can do to get around this potential hurdle. The easiest methods are to:

- Set up computers with internet access in your workplace where people can log in and respond. Select a quiet, private location with minimal distractions.

- ☐ Give your team the option of using their home PC. For example, give away 30 minutes paid time, let people leave early or come in late. Obviously you need to work within the confines of your specific policies, but there is always a way to make this happen. Rarely have I found this to be an issue.

- ☐ If you have employees that travel, they can login and complete the survey anywhere they can get an internet connection.

- ☐ If you have literacy challenges, you can modify your approach by hiring an outside administrative or temp service to enter the answers into your online survey. Team members can call in and provide their answers via telephone. You still get candid responses because respondents are still anonymous. You also still get the benefits of ease of reporting and quick results. If your budget will keep you from hiring a temp administrative service, consider using interns from a local community college or university. The key is to find a way to ensure candid responses.

Advantages of Web Survey Tools

- ☐ You can get results fast. Usually there is a peak in response rates right after you launch a survey. So, you are able to start seeing preliminary results within hours of launch.

- ☐ It's cost-effective. It doesn't matter whether you have five employees or 5,000. For most online services, the cost is the same.

- ☐ You can take advantage of built in logic to require answers to specific questions or allow respondents to skip questions that don't apply to them.

- ☐ You can set up anonymous responses but still get useful information about attitudes by job function or department so you can measure differences in attitudes across the organization and at different levels. (NOTE —You may want to skip this if it will compromise the anonymity and candor of your responses. For instance, if you have a very small team and identifying a respondent's job function would jeopardize their privacy).

- □ You have a graphical display that is easy for people to follow.
- □ You can add text introductions and messages to set a positive tone for the survey.
- □ On average, people provide longer answers to open-ended questions when responding online.
- □ It's flexible. You can use a variety of questioning methods such as multiple choice, yes/no, rank your preferences as well as open-ended questions.

Easy and Low Cost Employee Surveys

I have personally used two online survey tools that I can recommend. Both have advantages and disadvantages depending on what you need. You will want to select your best option based on your budget, and the features that are important to you. Please note; this information is current as of this writing. However, features and pricing can change, so please check their websites for current information about these services.

http://www.zoomerang.com They have a F*ree* and *Pro* version. Their free version allows you to do a basic 30-question survey using their templates or you can build one from scratch. However with their *Free* version, you only have 10 days to analyze your results and you can't download the reports. Their *Pro* option removes the 10-day limit and provides advanced reporting functions and tools such as download capabilities and the ability to import your email address book. It costs between $350 and $600 depending on your business status; they offer discounts for Non-profits and Education. Their primary advantages over Survey Monkey—they provide templates that you can use or edit and provide the ability to customize surveys in over 40 languages. You may want to test their *Free* version before purchasing, so you can see if you'll only need the features provided in the that version.

http://surveymonkey.com is a lower cost option. Their professional edition is just $20/month at the time of this writing. Their online tools and reporting are comparable to Zoomerang, but they don't offer templates. They do have a free version as well, but you are limited to 10 questions, 100 participants and won't have the reporting or advanced logic features. You also can't download your results with their free version, so it's worth the $20 to upgrade. There's also no long-term contract required, you can subscribe on a month-to-month basis unlike Zoomerang, which requires a one year commitment. Survey Monkey's primary disadvantage is they don't offer templates. But if you are using an existing survey or using a template provided with this program, you won't miss that feature.

Six Steps for Creating Powerful Surveys

STEP 1: Define the objective of your survey. Because your goal is to improve your organization's performance, you'll need to understand your team's current attitudes about your company and their job.

STEP 2: Compile email addresses or identify a strategy to reach everyone in your organization including managers, executives and staff. It's best to include all divisions or departments so you can compare differences in attitudes and performance by division, department and organizational hierarchy or job junction. *Again, be careful you do not compromise the integrity of your survey answers by asking respondents for information that could associate individuals with their survey answers.*

STEP 3: Select your tool or method of delivery. To get the fastest, most cost-effective and usable feedback, consider an online survey tool. If you don't like the options presented here, do a Google or Yahoo search on "employee surveys" to find alternatives to meet your needs.

STEP 4: Create your survey (see the example in this chapter). This is where you enter your questions into the online survey tool. This will be easier to do, if you create your survey first using your desktop word processing software prior to online set up. That way you can edit and just copy and paste into the online tool. You will also enter or upload your email addresses in this step. The online tools mentioned here provide that ability. When you launch, survey participants will receive an email with your message and a web link to your online survey.

STEP 5: Test, Refine and Launch. Have a few people take the survey online to check for usability and clarity. Prior to sending to all respondents, you will want to verify:

- □ The online survey works as intended.
- □ That respondents find it easy to understand and complete
- □ You've accurately estimated the time required to complete the survey.

You'll get the best feedback by testing with people who did not help you create the survey. The size of your test group will depend on your organization's size and the range of verbal comprehension across your organization. Refine your survey prior to sending your mass email announcement using the input you received from your test group. I usually like to have about seven to ten people test prior to launching. A test group of three will work as well.

The most important objective is to be certain your respondents will be able to understand and complete the survey, as intended, and in a reasonable amount of time.

STEP 6: Analyze your results. Now that you have completed your first survey—you have a benchmark! The results are a reflection of your team's beliefs and attitudes, which are driving your current performance results. So, now you know what needs to be fixed or fine tuned. This is a yardstick that will enable you to measure your progress going forward.

Other Best Practices

1. Include all business areas in your survey if possible. If you are responsible for company-wide morale and motivation, don't target one area without a good explanation or a plan to roll out every area. You may inadvertently raise suspicions about job cuts, or rumors about a group's performance. The human imagination can create destructive beliefs especially if

communication between managers and staff is not as good as it could be.

2. Don't provide too much time for people to respond as the tendency is to put it off until later. Response rates will suffer. Consider 3-4 working days with instructions for people on vacation to respond within 2-3 days of their return.

3. Enlist managers and executives to actively support and complete the survey. All members of management will need to communicate their support to get the best response rates. Some companies have contests, and acknowledge or reward departments that get 100% participation.

4, Create a high-powered message to communicate the importance of the survey. To get constructive feedback and good response rates—share the WIIFM (What's In It For Me) factor in addition to why it's important to the company. Then craft the message and get feedback from a few people at different levels in the organization. Revise and use this as your template to communicate a consistent, inspiring message to your organization. You'll use this message when you discuss why the survey is important, in the email you send to participants, and in your survey's introductory paragraph. Appeal to everyone's interests!

5. Communicate openly and honestly about why you are conducting the survey. If you know that the employees in your organization don't think that management values their opinion—don't lead off with, "We value your opinion" because you will instantly lose credibility. Be positive, but communicate that you know there are challenges. Leading off with—"As you know, we've had some recent challenges with (*customer satisfaction, quality, employee or turnover etc.)* and would like your opinion.." will communication far more sincerity.

6. Do something positive with the information as soon as the survey ends. If you delay, you lose the valuable energy and momentum you just created by asking people what they think and feel! Your follow up can be as simple as sending or posting

a message to thank everyone for their thoughtful answers. Tell your team about the next steps!

7. Continue to use the same survey to measure your progress. Your first survey becomes your benchmark—it's where you are today. Subsequent surveys allow you to measure your progress against where you started. In the first year, you'll want to monitor changes more frequently, perhaps; two to three times per year. After that, you can reduce the frequency until it becomes an annual activity. Reducing survey frequency can be tied to when you achieve your initial performance goals. However you should never cease surveying your employees. To do so may communicate that their opinions are no longer important and you will lose sight of the attitudes that drive your results.

A key to successful change is to keep your organization engaged throughout the process. Your communication does not have to be "high tech" or elaborate. But, you do need to keep your team members in the loop. Don't waste the valuable momentum and energy you can create—help your entire team (managers, staff, supervisors, executives, and possibly your vendors and suppliers) feel like they make a big difference in the success of your organization!

Sample Employee Satisfaction Surveys

There are two sample surveys included in this chapter. Sample I consists of 100 statements and uses a standard rating scale to measure employee attitudes about the ten areas that impact motivation and job satisfaction. A standard scale simplifies the analysis step. It is particularly useful if you have a large number of employees. This survey also reduces the natural biases that can occur due to individual word associations. It accomplishes this by using more than one question to measure attitudes about the same factor (such as commitment to customer satisfaction or trust in management etc).

You can adjust the length of this survey by choosing multiple questions from each of the ten categories listed.

Sample II is a shorter survey designed as a potential supplement or formatting option. It uses 20 questions in various formats, such as: multiple choice, yes/no, rating scales, and open-ended questions. It gives you actionable information, but the format provides less direct visibility to trends and patterns than a format with a standard rating scale (Sample I).

Survey Sample I is a good first step because it is designed to give you a comprehensive picture of your current workplace reality. It covers the ten areas that impact motivation, and is best suited for the SPIRIT six-step system. Remember, you can shorten template I to fifty to seventy-five questions if you want to create a shorter survey. Just be certain to include statements in each of the ten areas. Weigh the pros and cons of both formats, and customize a template that meets your specific needs.

Choose your survey carefully as you will be using it going forward to measure your progress. You'll want something that helps you easily gauge the effectiveness of your workplace/business improvement strategies. The survey information will also be used to help you prioritize your planned improvements based upon your biggest areas of need.

You can use these surveys as they are presented here, mix and match questions between the two surveys, tweak them, start from scratch, or use an exiting survey you might already be using.

Review and make adjustments to account for your organization's general mastery of the English language. Strive to use language that will appeal to the largest audience possible.

100 Sample Survey Statements

The information you gain through employee surveys helps you remove the obstacles that limit your potential. Survey data also allows you to quantify and forecast the bottom line impact of changing beliefs so you can see what's working well and what might need fine tuning.

Remember our outer world is a direct reflection of our inner world! So, surveys give you visibility to the beliefs and attitudes that determine your business results.

These survey statements will give you a solid view of the areas you will need to improve in order to create a highly motivated business team. They were designed to be used with this rating scale:

Strongly Agree | Agree | Somewhat Agree | Somewhat Disagree | Disagree | Strongly Disagree

The statements here are grouped into categories to help you choose the most appropriate statements for your organization. Use them to find out about the beliefs that drive your business success.

I. Customer Service Orientation at Your Company:

1. We listen closely to what our customers say.
2. Our actions tell our customers that they are important to us.
3. Customer satisfaction is a top priority at our (company, division, team, or department).
4. People here enjoy getting to know our customers.
5. Our (company, division, team, or department) leaders consistently communicate the needs of our customers.
6. We do a good job resolving customer issues when they occur.
7. The quality of customer service provided by my group is always excellent.
8. Most people in our (company, division, team, or department) do "whatever it takes" to make our customers happy.
9. We tell our customers about issues that might affect them.
10. We have a real commitment to high levels of customer service, and tolerate nothing else.
11. We excel at creating long-term customer relationships.
12. We always put our customers' needs first, ahead of those of the company.
13. If I were a customer instead of an employee, I would definitely buy from this company.
14. Our customers love doing business with us.
15. We have a good system for measuring customer satisfaction.
16. We regularly discuss the results of customer feedback.

17. We always find the best solutions to customer problems.

II. Empowerment at Your Company:

1. I can usually decide how to best complete my work.
2. Management here values ideas from all levels.
3. I have the opportunity to make the decisions necessary to do my job well.
4. I am encouraged to share ideas and suggestions for improving our business.
5. I understand how my work impacts the other people and processes in our business.
6. I understand my (company, division, team, or department) long-term goals. I know precisely what we want to achieve.
7. We are well informed about what is going on in our company.
8. I feel I have the management support I need to do my best work.
9. Employee suggestions are often implemented to improve how we operate our business.
10. Our policies and procedures help me make decisions that are good for our business.
11. Management trusts me to make the right decisions about how I perform my job.
12. My opinion is valued here.

III. Fair Compensation at Your Company:

1. Our compensation system encourages high quality work throughout the company.
2. I understand exactly how my performance determines my compensation.
3. The highest rewards go to those who best support the company's success.
4. I believe I am paid fairly for my contributions to the company.
5. The compensation system is managed fairly throughout the organization.
6. People are paid for the value they bring to the business.
7. Our compensation system is easy to understand.
8. I can directly influence the money I earn based on my contributions to the company.

IV. Quality of Products and Services at Your Company:

1. The quality of work in our (team, or department) is always first rate.
2. We are consistently committed to high quality work, and accept nothing less.
3. Our team always achieves our quality goals.
4. The quality in our company is as good as can be expected.
5. My manager recognizes a strong commitment to quality.
6. Our customers appreciate our dedication to quality.
7. I am encouraged to take immediate action to correct potential quality issues.
8. We are committed to ongoing quality improvement.
9. Our customers believe we provide high quality service.

V. Leadership Style at Your Company:

1. I feel comfortable talking to my manager about job related questions and concerns.
2. I think of my manager as more of a coach than a boss.
3. The people in my (group or department) consistently work well together as a team.
4. I enjoy working for my immediate supervisor. We have a good working relationship.
5. My manager is a good coach.
6. We are focused as a team on specific goals that help our company grow.
7. Management does a good job delegating work to the appropriate level.
8. We regularly discuss our progress toward company goals.
9. My manager displays an active interest in my ongoing development.
10. Team members and managers work together closely to create solutions that make our business and workplace better for everyone.
11. I feel appreciated and recognized for a job well done.
12. My manager does whatever he/she can to provide the tools and support I need to do my job well.
13. I belong to an enthusiastic team of people who work well together.
14. I know that my contributions are valued here.

15. We emphasize teamwork here. Behaviors that do not support the best interests of the team are not tolerated.

VI. High Standards at Your Company:

1. We prefer to be the best instead of the biggest.
2. We set and expect high standards of achievement here.
3. We are committed to excellence in everything we do.
4. Unsatisfactory job performance is not accepted here.
5. Customer projects are always managed with the highest degree of quality.
6. We go to great lengths to find the best people for every job.
7. We have no room for those who put their personal agenda ahead of the interests of the customers or company.
8. I am challenged by the amount of work I have, but I am not overwhelmed.
9. People throughout the company consistently give their very best work.
10. Divisions and departments work well together to provide the best possible service to our customers. Turf wars are not tolerated.

VII. Employee Satisfaction & Morale at Your Company:

1. I enjoy working here.
2. Most of my work is challenging.
3. I am proud of the work I do.
4. Our managers do what they say they will do. Management behaviors support the company goals.
5. I am satisfied with my job.
6. There are ample opportunities for career advancement at this company.
7. The management team listens well.
8. Employee morale and enthusiasm are very strong here.
9. People in our company always treat each other with respect. Disrespectful behavior is not tolerated.
10. There are many opportunities to grow and learn here.

VIII. Commitment, Enthusiasm and Respect at Your Company:

1. I feel my work has real meaning and significance.

2. If necessary, people put the needs of the company ahead of their own personal interests.
3. I openly discuss my opinions, even when others may disagree.
4. I believe the people here are committed to doing their best.
5. I feel plugged into what's happening in the company. Communication here is very good.
6. I trust the managers and executives who work here.
7. The management team inspires commitment and loyalty.
8. I would gladly recommend this company to my friends because it's a great place to work.
9. The managers here support a healthy work/life balance. I rarely if ever feel pressure from my manager to sacrifice my personal time.

IX. Long-Term Orientation at Your Company:

1. I understand our company mission.
2. Our company focuses on long-term success, not just short-term results.
3. A lot of the things we do will help our company succeed in the future.
4. There are real opportunities here for growth well into the future.
5. Our actions as a company consistently support the company's mission and values.

X. Training and Development at Your Company:

1. I have many opportunities to learn and develop new skills at work.
2. We are required to expand our work related skills.
3. I have the training I need to do my job extremely well.
4. The quality of the training here is very high.
5. The managers here make employee training a top priority.

Guidelines for Designing a Great Survey

- □ You can use every statement included in the sample survey or select a few from each category.

- □ Be consistent when using language to describe what area you want the respondents to consider as they answer each question. Where noted in the samples, select only one location depending on whether you are conducting the survey for a company, division, location or department. Use the term *department* or *group* when you are asking questions about coaching or trying to determine employee perceptions about the leadership abilities of their immediate supervisor.
- □ Randomize or mix your statements as you assemble your survey. In other words, don't ask for input about customer service, then employee satisfaction and morale etc. To promote candor, mix the statements. A complete template is included on the following pages.
- □ You will receive the best insights from first reactions as people read each question. So, encourage people in your written instructions to be frank and not to overanalyze. The first reaction most accurately reflects their honest beliefs. You will need to understand your current team's attitudes before you can improve motivation.

In *Practice What You Preach: What Managers Must Do to Create a High Achievement Culture*, David Maister maps employee attitudes to financial performance. He presents a compelling statistically-based case that employee beliefs and attitudes drive financial performance. He also provides a method for forecasting the impact of changes in employee attitudes. If you haven't read his book, I highly recommend you put it on your must-read list.

For more tips about survey design, see: http://www.surveysystem.com/sdesign.htm.

Survey Sample I

If you use every statement here, it will take about fifteen to twenty minutes for each respondent to complete the survey. Of course, timing will vary depending on individual reading and language skills. These statements are designed for this standard rating scale to make it easier for you to benchmark and then measure your progress going forward.

Strongly Agree | Agree | Somewhat Agree | Somewhat Disagree | Disagree | Strongly Disagree

> Thank you for taking the time to complete this survey. Your participation will help us create a better workplace for everyone!
>
> Please be candid and indicate your first reaction as you read each statement. Resist the temptation to overanalyze, simply go with your first choice'
>
> Your opinions are very important and your feedback will remain anonymous. You will not be asked to provide your name or contact information.
>
> You will need to allow about 15 to 20 minutes to complete the survey. Start in a quiet area and give yourself enough time to tell us what you think about each statement. You will not be able to stop and restart the survey. On the upcoming screen, you will be given a series of statements (*100 in all*). **Simply select the degree to which you agree or disagree on the scale provided.**
>
> **For each statement, your options are:**
>
> **Strongly Agree | Agree | Somewhat Agree | Somewhat Disagree | Disagree | Strongly Disagree**

1. I am encouraged to share ideas and suggestions for improving our business.

2. We are consistently committed to high quality work, and accept nothing less.

3. We listen closely to what our customers say.

4. I feel my work has real meaning and significance.

5. I understand our company mission.

6. Our actions tell our customers that they are important to us.

7. The quality of work in our (team, or department) is always first rate.

8. I enjoy working here.

9. There are many opportunities to grow and learn here.

10. Our company focuses on long-term success, not just short-term results.

11. I have the training I need to do my job extremely well.

12. My manager displays an active interest in my ongoing development.

13. Our policies and procedures help me make decisions that are good for our business.

14. Our team always achieves our quality goals.

15. Customer satisfaction is a top priority at our (company, division, team, or department).

16. We regularly discuss our progress toward company goals.

17. The quality in our company is as good as can be expected.

18. I am satisfied with my job.

19. People are paid for the value they bring to the business.

20. We are committed to excellence in everything we do.

21. People here enjoy getting to know our customers.

22. I feel comfortable talking to my manager about job related questions and concerns.

23. Our (company, division, team, or department) leaders consistently tell us about the needs of our customers.
24. We are well informed about what is going on in our company.
25. We are committed to ongoing quality improvement.
26. We set and expect high standards of achievement here.
27. My opinion is valued here.
28. I belong to an enthusiastic team of people who work well together.
29. The managers here make employee training a top priority.
30. I would gladly recommend this company to my friends because it's a great place to work.
31. The managers here support a healthy work/life balance. I rarely if ever feel pressure from my manager to sacrifice my personal time.
32. We do a good job resolving customer issues when they occur.
33. I can directly influence the money I earn based on my contributions to the company.
34. People in our company always treat each other with respect. Disrespectful behavior is not tolerated.
35. The quality of customer service provided by my group is always excellent.
36. Management trusts me to make the right decisions about how I perform my job.
37. Most people in our (company, division, team, or department) do "whatever it takes" to make our customers happy.
38. I understand my (company, division, team, or department) long-term goals. I know precisely what we want to achieve.

39. My manager does whatever he/she can to provide the tools and support I need to do my job well.

40. I feel plugged into what's happening in the company. Communication here is very good.

41. The management team inspires commitment and loyalty.

42. We tell our customers about issues that might affect them.

43. Our compensation system is easy to understand.

44. We emphasize teamwork here. Behaviors that do not support the best interests of the team are not tolerated.

45. I have many opportunities to learn and develop new skills at work.

46. We have a real commitment to high levels of customer service, and tolerate nothing else.

47. I have the opportunity to make the decisions necessary to do my job well.

48. I understand exactly how my performance determines my compensation.

49. My manager recognizes a strong commitment to quality.

50. Our customers believe we provide high quality service.

51. If necessary, people put the needs of the company ahead of their own personal interests.

52. Team members and managers work together closely to create solutions that make our business and workplace better for everyone.

53. I feel appreciated and recognized for a job well done.

54. We excel at creating long-term customer relationships.

55. The highest rewards go to those who best support the company's success.

56. We are focused as a team on specific goals that help our company grow.

57. The quality of the training here is very high.

58. Our actions as a company consistently support the company's mission and values.

59. We always put our customers' needs first, ahead of those of the company.

60. We prefer to be the best instead of the biggest.

61. Management does a good job delegating work to the appropriate level.

62. We go to great lengths to find the best people for every job.

63. We have no room for those who put their personal agenda ahead of the interests of the customers or company.

64. Employee morale and enthusiasm are very strong here.

65. The people in my (group or department) consistently work well together as a team.

66. Our customers appreciate our dedication to quality.

67. My manager is a good coach.

68. If I were a customer instead of an employee, I would definitely buy from this company.

69. I know that my contributions are valued here.

70. Our customers love doing business with us.

71. I can usually decide how to best complete my work.

72. I believe I am paid fairly for my contributions to the company.

73. Customer projects are always managed with the highest degree of quality.

74. People throughout the company consistently give their very best work.

75. I openly discuss my opinions, even when others may disagree.

76. I believe the people here are committed to doing their best.

77. I am challenged by the amount of work I have, but I am not overwhelmed.

78. I enjoy working for my immediate supervisor. We have a good working relationship.

79. I am proud of the work I do.

80. The management team listens well.

81. We have a good system for measuring customer satisfaction.

82. Employee suggestions are often implemented to improve how we operate our business.

83. We regularly discuss the results of customer feedback.

84. I understand how my work impacts the other people and processes in our business.

85. We always find the best solutions to customer problems.

86. Management here values ideas from all levels.

87. I am encouraged to take immediate action to correct potential quality issues.

88. Our compensation system encourages high quality work throughout the company.

89. Divisions and departments work well together to provide the best possible service to our customers. Turf wars are not tolerated.

90. Most of my work is challenging.

91. Our managers do what they say they will do. Management behaviors support the company goals.

92. Unsatisfactory job performance is not accepted here.

93. I feel I have the management support I need to do my best work.

94. The compensation system is managed fairly throughout the organization.

95. I think of my manager as more of a coach than a boss.

96. There are ample opportunities for career advancement at this company.

97. I trust the managers and executives who work here.

98. A lot of the things we do will help our company succeed in the future.

99. There are real opportunities here for growth well into the future.

100. We are required to expand our work related skills.

Please tell us where you work. (Select One: Accounting/Finance, Administration, Customer Service, Distribution, Human Resources, Inventory Management, Manufacturing, Marketing, Purchasing, Quality Control, Sales, Technology)

What is your job function? (Non-Supervisory Staff | Supervisor | Manager | Senior Management, Director or Vice President | Senior Executive, Chief Officer or Executive Vice President)

Thank you for completing this survey! We will be compiling the results so that we can work together to improve and grow. Look for more information in the near future.

Sincerely,

Insert Signature(s)*

* IMPORTANT: Seize the opportunity to create positive buzz and energy in your company! You will want to present the survey from a high-profile member of your management team such as your company President, CEO, Sr. VP of Operations. This will communicate a commitment from the highest level in the organization. Personally, I prefer adding the signatures of every member of the executive team such as the CEO, President, and top levels in Human Resources, Operations, Marketing, Finance and any other division you may have in your company. Doing this communicates urgency, importance and unity. Of course, you should review with the appropriate members of your executive team to gain buy-in.

Survey Sample II

The first sample provides you with a snapshot of respondent beliefs in the t*en specific areas of behavior that impact employee satisfaction and motivation*.

This template uses a variety of question and answer formats, rather than the standard rating scale used in Template I. The primary intent of Survey Sample II is to help you discover *perceptions* about the respondent's immediate supervisor and company benefits. So, you'll want to consider how that may impact your efforts to create positive change in your business. This survey can be a good supplementary tool if used with care. It's also included here to provide another format you can model when designing your survey.

> Thank you for taking the time to complete this survey. Your answers will help us continue to grow and improve!
>
> On the following screen, you will be asked a series of questions (twenty in all). Your answers will remain anonymous and we will not ask you for your name or contact information.
>
> Your answers and constructive comments will help us design programs that will help everyone work together better as a team.
>
> You will need to allow about ten to fifteen minutes to complete the survey. Start in a quiet area and give yourself enough time to provide comments as indicated. You will not be able to stop and restart the survey.
>
> On the upcoming screen, you will be given twenty questions. Please follow the instructions for each question, some ask for your comments, while others require a yes or no answer, or require you to indicate your level of agreement. **So, it's important that you read each question closely.**
>
> Thank you for your thoughtful feedback!

1. Overall, how SATISFIED are you with [COMPANY] as a place to work? (Select One: 1—Extremely Satisfied 2—Somewhat Satisfied 3—Satisfied 4—Somewhat *Un*satisfied 5-Extremely *Un*satisfied)

2. I understand the company's long-term goals. I know precisely what we want to achieve. (Select YES or NO)

3. Please describe our company mission and values as you understand them.

____

____

____

____

____

4. Do you have the tools and training you need to do your job well? (Select YES or NO)

5. Overall, do you think the management team consistently acts in the best interests of the company? (Select One: 1-Always | 2-Almost Always |3-Sometimes | 4-Almost Never | 5-Never)

6. In general, if you share your ideas with your supervisor, do you... (Select One:1-Get credit for offering an idea |2-Get credit only if an idea is implemented |3-Get no credit|4-N/A, I've never submitted an Idea or Suggestion)

7. I understand how my work impacts the other people and processes in our business. (Select YES or NO)

8. Indicate your level of AGREEMENT with the following statements about your immediate supervisor. (Indicate your thoughts in each area: 1—Strongly Agree 2—Somewhat Agree 3—Agree 4— Somewhat *Dis*agree or 5-Strongly *Dis*agree 6-N/A)

My boss:
a) Listens well
b) Is a good coach
c) Is knowledgeable about my work
d) Values my opinion
e) Does what he/she says he/she will do
f) Expects high standards
g) Gives me fair performance reviews
h) Keeps me informed about things that impact my work
i) Makes customer service a top priority in our area
j) Recognizes my contributions

9. Rate your AGREEMENT with the following statements about the company culture. (1—Strongly Agree 2—Somewhat Agree 3—Agree 4— Somewhat *Dis*agree or 5-Strongly *Dis*agree 6-N/A)

a) We have a strong work ethic here.
b) The people who provide the biggest contributions to the company are rewarded the most.
c) Overall, most people like working here.
d) We are a top performing company.
e) Customer satisfaction is a top priority here.
f) We work hard, but have fun too.
h) People treat one another with respect.
i) We are encouraged to continuously improve our skills.
j) Departments work well together. Turf wars are not tolerated.
k) Communication here is clear and effective.
l) High quality is a must; nothing less is accepted.

10. Please rate your SATISFACTION with the areas listed below. (Select One: 1—Extremely Satisfied 2—Somewhat Satisfied 3—Satisfied 4—Somewhat *Un*satisfied 5-Extremely *Un*satisfied 6-N/A)

a) Compensation
b) New hire orientation
c) Job training
d) Job description(s)
e) Performance reviews
f) Opportunities for advancement
g) Work hours/Flextime
h) Health care benefits
i) Retirement benefits

11. I can usually decide how to best complete my work. *(*Indicate your level of agreement here*:* (1—Strongly Agree 2—Somewhat Agree 3—Agree 4— Somewhat *Dis*agree or 5-Strongly *Dis*agree 6-N/A)

12. Have you ever offered a suggestion or idea to a member of management? (Select YES or NO)

13. If you have offered an idea or suggestion, to whom did you give the suggestion? (Select all that apply. If you have not offered an idea or suggestion, please go to the next question).

a) Immediate supervisor
b) Other member of management
c) Member of Human Resources or Personnel Department
d) Other, please specify ____________________

14. Do you enjoy working with the other people in your department? (Select YES or NO)

15. Do you think that most employees feel the same way you do about the company? (Select YES or NO)

16. Rate your AGREEMENT with the following statement. Our management team encourages high quality work throughout the entire company. (1—Strongly Agree 2—Somewhat Agree 3—Agree 4— Somewhat *Dis*agree or 5-Strongly *Dis*agree)

17. Do you have any suggestions about making this a better place to work? If so, please write them here.

____
____
____
____
____

18. How long have you been working for the company? (Less than a year | 1—2 years | 3—5 years | 6—10 years | More than 10 years)

19. I work in the following department: (Select One: Accounting/ Finance, Administration, Customer Service, Distribution, Human Resources, Inventory Management, Manufacturing, Marketing, Purchasing, Quality Control, Sales, Technology)

20. What is your job function? (Non-Supervisory Staff | Supervisor | Department Manager | Senior Management, Director or

Vice President | Senior Executive, Chief Officer or Executive Vice President)

Thank you for your feedback, we really want to make this a great place to work!

Sincerely,

Insert Signature(s)*

Again, seize the opportunity to create positive buzz and energy in your company! You will want to present the survey from high-profile members of your management team such as your company president, CEO, Sr. VP of Operations. This will communicate a commitment from the highest levels in the organization.

Communicating Value

As with any change or improvement effort, you'll want to communicate the value to your team on both a personal and professional level. A well-designed survey provides information that can benefit everyone in your organization in a very meaningful way. As the health of your workplace grows stronger:

1. Your organization's potential expands dramatically
2. Possibilities for career advancement and growth increase
3. Creativity soars
4. Job satisfaction improves
5. Mutual respect grows
6. Work takes on more meaning
7. Operating costs go down as productivity and quality improve
8. You attract and retain more ideal customers
9. You have a healthier bottom line
10. Fire fighting diminishes
11. The bottom line can support more or better compensation programs and benefits
12. Your job gets easier
13. Opportunities for life balance expand

14. Community perception of your company improves
15. You attract more ideal employees
16. Your shareholders are happier
17. The overall quality of life can get better for everyone
18. Opportunities for long term growth and sustainability improve dramatically

There are far more benefits, but this should get you thinking about the personal and professional value of a healthy business culture. Keep this list of eighteen benefits handy as you prepare communication about workplace improvement, or the value of a stronger culture. Please notice that I did not use the term "employee motivation program". For to do so in your communication, could mistakenly convey that this effort is to correct a personal character flaw. Nothing could be further from the truth!

Workplace health is a direct result of cumulative thinking, attitudes, and actions that have occurred over a long period of time. So, improvement is not about finding fault. It is about coming together to create an extraordinary workplace and business! Present your efforts as a means to strengthen and condition your business. Consider the words you choose carefully from all perspectives so your communication is perceived in the highest light possible.

Communicate "what's in it for me" to everyone, personally as well as professionally. If you do so, you will be well on your way to engaging your entire team on a grand journey.

Performance Trends and Workplace Health

You can tell a lot about the health of your organization by reviewing your company's performance data. If you compare trends across locations, departments, and by manager, you can gain valuable insights about the leadership style and degree of employee satisfaction in each area.

By comparing business units in your company, you can also find out who and what is working well as you design and implement your workplace improvement program. Of course you'll want to account for transfers in leadership to ensure you are associating performance results with the appropriate manager or supervisor.

During step 1, you will work with the data you have. *Don't get stuck here if your data is less than perfect.* You can add better reporting systems later. Here are **K**ey **P**erformance **I**ndicators (KPIs) you can use to assess your workplace's current strengths and weaknesses.

- □ Employee Satisfaction Survey Scores
- □ Absenteeism (*company, division and manger/supervisor)*
- □ Production output/employee (*company, division and manger/ supervisor)*
- □ Voluntary turnover rates (*company, division and manger/ supervisor*)
- □ Non-voluntary turnover rates (*company, division and manger/ supervisor*)
- □ Quality ratings (*company, division and manger/supervisor)*
- □ Exit Interviews (voluntary and non voluntary)
- □ Customer satisfaction scores
- □ Net profits/employee (*company, division and manger/ supervisor)*
- □ Sales trends (*Are you moving up or down? Are the results eradicate or steady? What recent changes impact your trends? Do you have a new competitor? Do your sales trends mirror trends in other areas? Are you in the midst of a rapidly changing market? Did you implement a recent price change? How are your quality scores trending? Have you made any recent promotional changes or budget changes?*)

TO GET A GOOD ASSESSMENT OF CAUSE AND AFFECT, PERFORMANCE METRICS SHOULD BE LOOKED AT HOLISTICALLY.

Here's an example of how you might compare different trends to identify root cause.

Your sales have declined 15% from the same period last year. That by itself doesn't tell you much. So you speak with the Marketing Manager and learn that: promotional spending is actually up over last year, there are no changes in pricing or industry demand, and there are no new competitors in the market.

You review your customer defective returns and find that as a percentage of sales, your customer return rate is the same as last year. However, your customer traffic is down.

So, you review your customer satisfaction scores and find that score has declined by 22%. Your review indicates that your customers are waiting longer for service although there are no changes to staffing. Your customers are defecting to a long-time competitor. *Now what?*

You've got your employee satisfaction survey scores and by reviewing your results, you find that only 30% of the respondents agree that customer satisfaction is your company's top priority. If you had a survey from a previous period (say six months ago) you may find that 50% agreed that customer service was your company's top priority. Although that score wasn't perfect, it's getting worse instead of better.

You look at the quality scores and you learn those are declining as well, but output/employee is up.

So, now you know what you need to do. You need to find the actions that are not aligned with your #1 priority - Exemplary Customer Service.

After reviewing your survey results and speaking with some managers and employees, you find the culprits. The drive to expand your market share has created the perceptions that *bigger* is more important than *best.* Managers and employees focused too much attention on employee throughput at the expense of quality and customer service follow up and communication. NOW you can correct the problem.

This is the power of employee surveys, they are easy to do and they can fill in the gaps you may have from less than perfect data.

Performance trend data doesn't always give you the complete picture and because it's usually not stored in a central location it can be time consuming to pull together.

Use the performance data you have today to get started and your employee survey results. Don't get stuck here trying to create the perfect reporting system. That will only delay the benefits of improved employee morale.

You can fill in your data gaps with the results from your survey and by speaking with your informal leaders.

As you move forward, you will want to partner with other resources in your company to get a system in place that will help you measure, monitor, and align your compensation and reward systems with your evolving objectives.

For now, just remember...*Energy flows where attention goes* and *you can't manage that energy if you don't measure it!*

Connect with Your Informal Leaders

Every organization has informal leaders. These are the employees or managers whom other employees or managers go to for advice or input. These are the folks who shape opinions and can influence the attitudes and beliefs of other people within their sphere of influence.

Informal leaders may or may not be functional managers. They are often long-term employees who understand the big picture. They know how processes work across departments and understand how to get things done in your organization. Another sign of an informal leader—find out where your new hires go to learn the lay of the land.

Chances are you know who your informal leaders are. You can also check with the managers who have strong communication networks throughout your organization. These are the leaders in your organization who are closest to your employees. So, they can tell you how they keep their finger on the pulse of the organization.

Why do you want to speak with your informal leaders?

- □ You can gain *qualitative* insights into what is affecting your motivation and morale.
- □ You may pick up new ideas or insights that you can include in your improvement program.
- □ You want to understand their beliefs and attitudes. Because they exercise influence—you want to know where they fit into your next steps. If you have an informal leader who has a positive perspective about the company, he/she may be a great change agent. These folks can create a lot of enthusiasm and energy to support you in your efforts to create a better workplace.
- □ You'll also want to know who might throw up road blocks so you can help them get on-board or get out of your way.
- □ Informal leaders have the power to influence (for better or worse), so you'll want to gauge where they are.

This part of the process is not elaborate. Just take these five steps:

1. Identify your informal leaders.

2. Call them and schedule time to meet individually. You may want to share that you are getting ready to start a project to help improve the quality of the employee's workplace experience. You've heard that they are well respected *or* they've been a valuable part of the team for x years and you'd like to hear their opinions. *Make sure they are comfortable meeting with you.* If not, ask if they can tell you why. If they are not willing to share, don't push it. Thank them and go on to the next person on your list.

3. Meet. Provide a little background about what you want to accomplish before asking your questions. You want to create a relaxed atmosphere and certainly don't want your interviewee to feel like he/she is being interrogated. Confirm that the information he/she will share will help the company grow both financially and culturally. You may want to convey that

their feedback will be confidential if you think that will enable better feedback. If that's the case, then be prepared to guard that trust! If you lose someone's trust, you may never regain it. The objective here is to find out what's broken, not to assign blame. The source of the information is not important—the hidden opportunity within the message is.

4. Listen and take notes. You'll be doing the listening here, ask and avoid the temptation to interject your opinions. A best practice is to ask permission prior to taking notes to help the interviewee feel valued and at ease.

5. Compile your notes and look for common themes. Your common themes tell you what the universal issues are across your organization. Common themes are important because they tend to be major obstacles and may be your top priority as you implement your program. You'll prioritize in the *Reflect and Design* step. This is where you compare the gaps between your current situation (what you discover in the Survey step) with your vision of your *Perfect Workplace* (what you create in step three).

The number of people you interview or the length of the interview is not important. Get a good cross section of departments if you can. Remember the benefits you gain with one-on-one discussions are:
- □ The valuable insights you receive AND
- □ The positive energy and trust you are starting to build.

There's no magic number, but you'll want to start with the folks that are connected with the inner workings of your organization and people you feel can give you the best insights into employee satisfaction.

Generally, I like to keep the interviews to about twenty to thirty minutes and use open ended questions. Here are some questions to get you started:

- □ How would you describe the morale here?

- ☐ Why would you describe it this way? Or, without using names or divulging a confidence, what general behaviors or actions have you observed that lead to your opinion?

- ☐ If you could change or improve anything—what would you start with? Why would you start there?

- ☐ If this were your company, what would you change or do to improve the way we do business?

- ☐ Would you say that morale has changed recently? How long would you say it's been as you describe it?

Tips for Sharing Survey Results

Managers, Business Owners, Executives and Human Resources Professionals—you need an accurate picture of your reality today if you are going to remove the barriers that keep your organization from reaching its full potential.

Setting realistic expectations about this step is so critical that it's worth mentioning twice. As I mentioned before…I have been surprised by the number of very intelligent and caring leaders who closed off critical communication streams simply because they didn't like the message and reacted poorly. As the saying goes; don't shoot the messenger.

Here's a fact—some of the information you may discover may be painful to hear. However, you cannot discover your opportunities without also seeing your areas that need improvement. You will also find there are some things working better than others.

Avoid the urge to sugarcoat the results by over-emphasizing the positives. Of course point out what is working well, but be direct about the areas that require improvement. Let your managers know up front that you will share the results and, as leaders, you expect them to receive the information openly. There is no such thing as BAD NEWS! These insights give you opportunities to take your organization beyond what you may currently be able to imagine.

Set some ground rules up front so your managers can prepare themselves before you share the results of your assessment.

1. Focus on the value of the message, not the messenger.

2. It's impossible to fix a problem if you don't understand what's broken.

3. Don't take things personally. Your current situation evolved over time with contributions from everyone on the leadership team. Everyone owns the current results. Together we can learn, grow and excel!

4. You can't fix problems with the same thinking that created it in the first place. Challenge your managers and supervisors to step out of their comfort zones. They can't keep doing the things they are doing and expect different results.

5. Remind everyone of the benefits of improving employee motivation and morale. Ask: *What would improved productivity, higher sales, lower employee turnover, employee enthusiasm mean to you personally and professionally?* If you take the time to really consider the implications—it's huge. I usually hear things like:

- □ I'd have less stress.
- □ I'd be in a better mood.
- □ I'd have more time to work on long-term planning because I'd be spending less time putting out fires.
- □ I'd have more time with my family.
- □ I'd make more money and get bigger bonuses.
- □ I'd be able to take that vacation I've been dreaming about.
- □ I'd actually look forward to coming to work.

You get the idea—help your leaders focus on the desired result for them personally as well as what's in it for the company!

Set the expectations up front that some parts of your assessment (particularly the survey results) may be hard to hear. But, it's an absolute necessity if you are going to achieve your mission critical goals and create an ideal workplace! An ideal workplace is one that supports your highest goals, loftiest dreams and produces a top performing company.

Everything you do in this step will help you identify the gaps between where you are today and where you want to be. The information will help you identify what you need to do to get the results you want both culturally and financially. You cannot separate the two—your culture and bottom line performance are interconnected. Change one and you impact the other!

Now, let's move to step two—planning for success!

Chapter 4 | Step 2: Planning for Success

"All you need is the plan, the road map, and
the courage to press on to your destination."

~ *Earl Nightingale*

Most business failures can be attributed to taking action without the critical act of planning. In the words of Benjamin Franklin, "By failing to prepare, we prepare to fail." Planning makes the dream work.

The word *plan* seems to imply that the process is a one-time proposition. However, a good plan evolves over time to reflect changing conditions. A plan gets better as it is updated to reflect your business conditions and the lessons you learn along the way. An effective plan requires an effective planning process.

In the *Motivation-at-Work* system, you begin with the *Survey.* In step one; you engaged your entire business team to gain absolute clarity about where your organization is today. This Survey step helps you:

- □ Establish the root causes for underperformance.
- □ Identify the specific areas that need improvement, and
- □ Prioritize your actions to achieve your desired benefits faster.

Let's look at how *Step 2, Planning for Success, fits into the six step Motivation-at-Work system.*

Survey ⇨ Plan ⇨ Imagine ⇨ Reflect & Design ⇨ Inspire ⇨Transform

Survey. You assess your current situation. You identify root causes of underperformance. You discover what's broken and what is working well when you complete this step. You'll understand the underlying beliefs that are driving your business results. Your first survey is a baseline. You'll also use the survey to measure the results of the strategies you implement as you move through the subsequent steps.

Plan. You will learn about the critical planning process and discover some tools that will help you achieve your objectives faster. You'll create a plan designed specifically for your organization's needs and goals as you proceed though each step.

Imagine. In this step, you create your *Perfect Workplace Vision* and *Goals*. Your goals will be **S**pecific, **M**easurable, **A**ttainable, **R**elevant, and **T**ime-based (SMART). Your vision helps you inspire your team to grow. Your vision is your compass that allows you to make decisions that are aligned with your transformation objectives. You create a plan to help you achieve the goals you develop in this step.

Reflect & Design. In this step, you compare your goals (*which reflect your desired future state*) with your survey results (*which reflect your current state*). This step identifies the gaps between where you are now, and where you want to be. When you *Design*, you choose the strategies that close your gaps, so you can create the *Top Performing Business* and *Perfect Workplace* you envision.

Inspire your Managers. In this step, you review your leadership development needs. You pick the strategies that work best for your organization, and update your plan. This step helps you develop an effective approach for transforming the single biggest area of impact to your transformation efforts.

Transform. This is where you implement your strategies and continue to monitor your progress. In this step, you are continuously improving and refining your approach. You'll update your plan, check off items as you complete them, and add new ones.

As you move through each step, you will update your plan based on what you've learned and accomplished. Your plan will reflect your specific vision, needs and goals. As you work through each step, we will identify potential obstacles and critical dependencies. By doing this, you will minimize delays, save time and money, and achieve your desired outcomes faster and with fewer headaches.

In this chapter you will learn:

- ☐ The *10-Point Planning System*
- ☐ How to clarify your objectives so you can effectively communicate the desired outcomes to your company leaders
- ☐ A simple planning template that will help you keep your transformation efforts on track
- ☐ How to diffuse the seven common areas of failure
- ☐ How to keep issues from managing you and your team
- ☐ The *Key Transformation Roles*
- ☐ How to handle resource constraints
- ☐ How to use team standards to help you select your team
- ☐ Nine tips to achieve results faster
- ☐ Where to find more help with the planning process

Plan Your Work; Work Your Plan

As you plan, you'll be using proven project management techniques that will help you coordinate the necessary steps and resources to transform your organization. I've simplified these processes, so you can spend more time implementing the benefit-rich strategies, and less time figuring out the tools. We'll lay out the sequence of events that need to occur so you can achieve your *Perfect Workplace* and *Top Performing* goals.

As you work your plan, you effectively manage the people, resources and activities you need to reach your desired destination.

The most important part of meeting objectives and deadlines is to start with a well-defined plan. As you go through each step in the six-step process you'll continue to develop your plan.

Keep It Simple. You can spend hundreds of hours learning the art and science of project management. There are also expensive programs that track activities and resource time in painstaking detail. That is not the intention with the *10-Point Checklist*.

Plans do not have to be perfect to be effective. In fact, a good plan that helps you gets results faster is far better than a "perfect plan" that never gets you off the ground.

You can get stuck in the planning process if you try to anticipate every possible task and contingency. That's critical if you are building a space shuttle or implementing high-impact technology or process changes. However, an effective planning tool for most business improvement initiatives is simply a detailed checklist. It is not necessary to learn how to create detailed Gantt charts or Work Breakdown Structures unless, of course, you are building a space shuttle or implementing a series of process changes that can have significant operational or financial repercussions. There are additional resources listed later in this chapter, if you feel you need more help in this area.

The *10-Point Planning Checklist* provides you with a basic process for effectively organizing and managing your transformation efforts. Each step in the *Motivation-at-Work* system is aligned with the act of planning. So, you'll also receive planning reminders and additional tips and strategies as you complete each step.

The 10-Point Planning Checklist

1. Define your objectives. First, identify your intentions for motivating your employees. This is the first thing on the checklist because it defines the *why*. We need to know *why* before we can define *what we will do* and *how we will do it*. An exercise in this chapter will help you clarify your objectives so you can effectively communicate the desired outcomes to your company leaders.

2. Identify your available resources and any constraints that may impact your schedule. Constraints are things like scheduled vacation time, other projects, or missing skills. Typical ways to address resource constraints are to adjust your timeline, reprioritize other work, simplify a task or strategy, or add resources to hit your target completion dates.

3. Create goals that enable you to achieve your desired outcomes. We'll cover this in depth in the Imagine chapter.

4. Break your goals into smaller pieces or tasks. You'll do this when you add goals, actions and strategies to your plan.

5. Assign resources that are best suited to each task.

6. Assign target completion dates for each task.

7. Manage your dependencies and resource availability. The dependencies are the activities you need to complete before another activity can start. As you add tasks to your plan, you'll want to allow sufficient time between dependent tasks to minimize delays. To meet your target completion dates, check resource workload to ensure team members can reasonably accomplish what you assign to them. A best practice is to work with your team to determine completion dates.

8. Monitor and follow up to get progress reports before task due dates. If you follow up before task due dates, you'll be able to resolve issues before they delay your desired outcomes.

9. Track and resolve issues. Inevitably problems surface as you make changes in an organization. There is a simple process you can use to keep those issues from taking people's attention away from what is important now. You'll get the details under "Manage the Issues" in this chapter.

10. Continue to review, refine, and update your plan. This is the difference between *planning* and a *plan.* Your approach will shift as your workplace transforms and as business conditions change. This is an important distinction because a plan is meant to be worked. The process of working the plan is what moves you closer to your goals.

Provide Purpose with Objectives

This is a very simple exercise designed to help you connect with your most important objectives. When you move to the next chapter, you'll work with your team to refine your objectives into a vision and specific goals. Give yourself twenty to thirty minutes to answer the following five questions now. By spending the time to gain clarity here, you position yourself to create a message that gets your team energized and moving in the same direction.

1. What are the benefits you want to achieve? For example, are you concerned most with improving productivity? Quality? Customer satisfaction? Sales? Employee commitment? Workplace enthusiasm? What does a *Perfect Workplace* look like to you? *Think big and shoot for the moon. Small improvements won't keep you or anyone else inspired for long.*

2. What are your biggest pains or problem areas today?

3. If you were able to fix each of these problems, what would that mean to you *personally*?

4. If you were able to fix each of the problems you identified in question 2, what would that mean to your business?

5. If you had to choose your top three priorities, what would they be and why?

When you complete this exercise, you'll have a snapshot of your workplace objectives or desired outcomes. This is a starting point. Enlist the support and help of your team to complete the vision and goal setting process in the *Imagine* step.

If you actively engage your team, you'll build ownership and commitment because your team members will feel they have an active part in the solution. You will reduce resistance to new ideas and changes when you engage others in solving problems. Also, ideas and strategies become more robust and far more effective when we add other people's perspectives to the creative processes. If we try to lock in the *how* too quickly, or make key decisions in a vacuum, we can close ourselves off to better alternatives.

A Simple Planning Template

The table on the next page is a simple template you can use to help you effectively record and track the tasks that will help you achieve your *Top Performing Business* and *Perfect Workplace* goals. This is a planning tool you can update as you proceed through each of the six steps.

Let's review each of the column headings on the next page.

#—Number you can assign to tasks to help you quickly identify a specific item as you review your plan with your team.

Task Description—A short definition of an activity that is on your plan. Activities on your plan help you reach your goals and vision.

Desired Outcome—The primary benefit you expect to achieve for each task. This clarifies the expected end result.

Owner —The individual that will manage and/or complete the task.

Other Resources—Additional people who will help the person responsible complete the task. Not all tasks will require supporting resources. You can also use this column to record supplies you need to acquire to complete each task.

Complete On—The target completion date.

Comments/Sign-Off/Review—Add information if needed for clarification. This is where you would indicate the need for a team review, manager sign off or committee approval.

Planning Template

#	Task Description	Desired Outcome	Owner	Other Resources	Complete On	Comments / Sign-Off /Review

The S.P.I.R.I.T. Plan

The following project list outlines the supporting tasks for each of the six steps in the *Motivation-At-Work* system. Each item in bold font is a major step forward in the plan. The tasks below the major steps are the actions required to complete that milestone. You can use this plan to help you organize and manage your transformation goals and objectives. You'll be adding your unique strategies as you proceed through each step.

Progress is made with each step forward. Don't let the number of tasks discourage you. This system was designed to help you start realizing the benefits of increased employee commitment and enthusiasm as you move through each task. So, you don't have to wait until you've completed each major milestone to realize improvements in your workplace.

S Survey - Assess your Current Situation
S1 Read the Survey Chapter
S2 Define Your Survey Objectives
S3 Choose and/or Refine Your Survey
S4 Gather Respondent Contact Information
S5 Review, Test & Refine Your Survey
S6 Launch your Survey
S7 Analyze Your Results

P Plan - Prepare for Success
P1 Read the Plan Chapter
P2 Define Your Primary Objectives
P3 Review Your Resource Needs and Get Your Team Ready
P4 Use the Tools & Strategies in this Chapter to Help You Reach Your Goals Faster

IM Imagine - Create Your Vision & Goals. Minimize Obstacles.
IM1 Read the Imagine Chapter
IM2 Identify Your Imagine Team Members
IM3 Create & Select Your Top 10 Perfect Workplace Attributes
IM4 Create & Select Your Top 10 Perfect Workplace Employee Contributions
IM5 Create Your Perfect Workplace Vision
IM6 Create Your SMART Goals

IM7 Identify Potential Obstacles & Create a *No Roadblocks Plan* to Diffuse Them
IM8 Use Your Vision, Goals & No Roadblocks Strategies to Keep You on Track

R Reflect & Design - Fill in the Gaps with Strategies to Achieve Your Goals.
R1 Read the Reflect & Design Chapter
R2 Identify Your Design Team Members
R3 Review Surveys & Current Performance Results
R4 Identify the Gaps between Your Current State and Your Perfect Workplace Vision and Goals
R5 Select or Adapt the Strategies to Close Your Gaps
R6 Prioritize the Strategies to Maximize Your Change Benefits
R7 Update Your Plan with Your Strategy and Target Dates

IN Inspire - Energize & Develop Your Leaders.
IN1 Read the Inspire Chapter
IN2 Identify Priorities for Growth Based On Survey Results
IN3 Integrate Enlightened Leader Behaviors
IN4 Engage Your Managers to Design Their Development Program
IN5 Select Your Leadership Development Strategies
IN6 Map Your Manager Selection Process to Enlightened Leader and Top Performance Behaviors
IN7 Align Your Manager Evaluation and Compensation Approach to Support Enlightened Leader and Top Performance Behaviors
IN8 Review Other Resources Chapter and add Strategies that Support Continuous Improvement
IN9 Update Your Plan

T Transform - Create continuous improvements
T1 Read the Transform Chapter
T2 Merge Cultural Health Metrics with Your Business Rhythms
T3 Align Companywide Performance & Selection Processes to Make Changes Stick
T4 Teach the Continuous Improvement Transformation Process to Your Managers and Leaders
T5 Continue to use the *Motivation at Work System, Website, & Resources* for Help
T6 Update & Refine Your Plan for Ongoing Improvement & Growth

Diffuse the 7 Common Areas of Failure

Sometimes the only difference between success and failure is knowing the common risks that can take you off track. When you understand the conditions that can keep you from achieving your goals, you can build a plan that diffuses these potential obstacles.

In the following table are seven common circumstances that can keep you from creating a *Perfect Workplace* and *Top Performing Business*. Each risk area includes suggested strategies to help you reduce their potential impact. The *Motivation-at-Work* system was designed to help you maximize the success of your transformation efforts by reducing the possible roadblocks.

#	Risks	Mitigate By
1	Too many projects or initiatives with no coordinated rollout strategy can dilute your results.	Complete each step in the *Motivation-at-Work* System in the appropriate order. This helps you effectively prioritize your time and resources. Create your plan, and work your plan.
2	Inadequate representation and input from every area. This amplifies change resistance. Incomplete information can send you down the wrong path or reduce your benefits.	Survey every employee including managers, executives, and team members. Use the approaches in the *Motivation-at-Work* system to conduct brainstorming sessions and discovery meetings with representatives from every area of your business.
3	Inadequately defining roles and responsibilities early in the transformation process.	Follow the planning process. Distribute and work your plan. Assign responsibilities based on skills needed. Partner people to maximize your team strengths. Confirm each team member understands desired outcomes for assigned tasks. Communicate key roles (Steering Committee, Project Manager etc.) in writing and verbally.
4	Underestimating the impact of human nature to preserve old processes and behaviors and resist new ones.	Communicate What's In It For Me (WIIFM) as well as how the business benefits. Communicate the price of doing nothing. Highlight success stories. Recognize and reward people who volunteer and adopt changes quickly.

#	Risks	Mitigate By
5	Unstructured approach can delay results or negatively impact performance in other areas of your business.	Regularly monitor project schedule. Track sliding tasks, and make date changes or add resources as needed. Ask for status reports from people who are managing multiple improvement initiatives.
6	Insufficient commitment or review by senior executives for high impact strategies and issues.	Identify Steering Committee Members, secure agreement for objectives, time requirements and heir role.
7	Your workplace improvement efforts may suffer from low credibility. This is when a team lacks faith that anything will really change. These beliefs are influenced by past events such as initiatives your employees consider ineffective, workforce downsizing, or incongruent management behaviors.	Build trust and engagement by using or adapting the strategies outlined in this system. Get team members throughout your organization involved in shaping your workplace. Ask for feedback and be very responsive to concerns. Acknowledge past failures and then move on. Consistently communicate the benefits of moving forward. Your past does not dictate your future unless you let it.

Manage the Issues so They Don't Manage You

An issue is a potential problem such as an ineffective process, limiting belief, unsupportive behavior, or resource constraint that could negatively impact your workplace transformation efforts. It is not uncommon for people to get sidetracked or overwhelmed by issues that surface as you make changes.

If issues are not managed properly, they can significantly delay your results or may resurface in the future as a major barrier.

Simply log issues as they surface to keep your team focused on actions that move them closer to your objectives. Don't worry about trying to resolve every issue as it is identified, or you'll get side tracked by things that don't need to be a priority now. Just write it down in an *Issue Log.* A template is included in this chapter to help you effectively manage issues, so they don't manage you. The template helps you review issues on your schedule so you can determine if you need to deal with them sooner, later, or never.

Enlist help from people on your team to help you resolve the issues. If the problem is related to an ineffective process or procedure, get input from the people who are closest to that process or procedure. They are often in the best position to resolve issues.

Assign issue resolution dates giving yourself ample time to resolve them, so they don't inadvertently delay the completion of an important task or milestone. Review and work the *Issue Log* regularly. Don't worry about trying to solve every problem right away. Concentrate on the high pay-off areas or the low hanging fruit first.

Use the following template to help you effectively track and resolve any issues that surface during your transformation process.

CAUTION—Sometimes sensitive issues surface that are related to an individual's job performance. Your *Issue Log* should not be used to track problems related to individual personnel related issues or behaviors unless you take the necessary measures to ensure confidentiality, security, and privacy. Coach your transformation team about applicable laws and your specific policies for handling personnel related issues. Only share sensitive information as dictated by your legal counsel, or as outlined by your Human Resources professional.

ISSUE LOG Template

Last Updated :_______________

KEY: Status: O=Open A=Assigned R=Resolved C=Approved & Closed D=Deferred N=No Action Priority: C=Critical H=High M=Medium L=Low

#	Description	Identified By	Assigned to	Priority	Resolve by Date	Status	Resolution

Issue Log Instructions

- ☐ Any team member may raise or identify an issue or potential obstacle.

- ☐ Update the *Issues Log* when a potential issue is identified. Record a brief description, the name of person identifying (in case you need to clarify) and possible resolution if known.

- ☐ A Project Manager or designated individual reviews the *Issue Log* on a regular basis to assign the priority. Usually a weekly review is sufficient, but you may want to review more frequently at the beginning of the project, or request *Critical* issues be brought to your attention immediately. The priorities are: **C=Critical** (Significant and immediate impact to the success of your transformation objectives) **H=High** (Significant impact, but does not require immediate attention) **M=Medium** (May minimize the desired benefits, but does not require attention at this time) **L=Low** (Minimal impact on the success or desired outcomes of the transformation program)

- ☐ The Project Manager, or designated individual, assigns a status. The default status for all newly logged issues is **O=Open** which means it has only been logged and not yet assigned for further research. **A=Assigned** means that someone has been given the responsibility of identifying options for resolution. **R=Resolved** indicates that a workable solution has been identified. **C=Approved & Closed** means the resolution has been approved by the appropriate person or committee and the resolution is noted in the log. **D=Deferred** means the issue will remain on the log but research and assignment can occur at a later date, **N=No Action** means that no resolution is required.

- ☐ The Project Manager, or designated individual, assigns someone to investigate possible solutions, or may assign himself/herself if he/she is in the best position to resolve the issue. At this time, a *resolve by* date is assigned based on the priority of the issue. Typically critical and high priority issues are assigned for resolution before a medium or low priority issue because they have greater impact on the outcome and may affect the completion date of a near term task.

- ☐ Require Sponsor or Steering Committee approval for complex issues. These are problems that may have a significant impact on your organization, operational or financial results, budget, or operations or policies. However, you don't want to stifle innovative thinking either, so choosing Steering Committee members that are open-minded and solution-focused will be critical to the success of your transformation efforts.

- ☐ If no action is needed, note a brief explanation in the resolution column and close with an N for No Action. This will help you remember why no action was need should a similar issue surface in the future.

A Few Words About Your Budget

Most of the strategies included in the program are ideas that provide maximum impact at minimal cost. So cost depends on the strategies and ideas you choose to implement.

To determine your potential return, refer to the objectives you created in this chapter. Review your biggest pains or problem areas. What would it mean to you and your business if you resolved these problems? If you need more help identifying potential benefits, refer to the list of benefits outlined in introductory chapter of this program book.

What would a 5% increase in productivity be worth to you? What about 15% or 40%? Consider the impact on the quality of your products or services. How does declining quality impact your bottom line? What does it cost you every time one of your key team members leaves your company? What is the lifetime value of your customers? How does employee turnover impact your customer retention rate? What is that costing your company?

There is no limit to the potential returns to your business when you create a committed, enthusiastic and respectful workplace. Every step you take to create a *Perfect Workplace* moves you closer to the benefits that come with a *Top Performing Business*.

Building a Team for Transformation

As you get ready to transform your business, you'll want to consider how you get your team involved in the transformation process. Understanding some key roles and responsibilities will help you determine who to engage.

The roles outlined here don't imply a one-to-one relationship. In other words, one individual may have two roles, such as the Transformation Architect and Sponsor.

How you decide to assign the roles will depend on the size of your organization, your available resources, individual skills, and the scope of the changes you want to make in your organization. You should adjust or combine responsibilities to meet your unique needs.

The Key Roles

The following roles are the functions that need to occur during a successful transformation. This does not mean you'll need to hire additional staff, unless you want to. That decision is dependent upon your budget, available resources and strengths, and your need for speed.

Many successful transformations occur using the resources within the existing organization. However, effective transformation does require that the people with the most influence on your desired outcomes, have or are open to developing the necessary skills to fulfill their transformation responsibilities.

As you read through each role, consider who you have on your team that has exhibited the strengths and skills required for that role. You may find this is a great opportunity to further develop the natural talents of some of the people on your team.

The Transformation Architect

The architect utilizes everyone's strengths to build something extraordinary. Like an architect, he or she consults with builders, tradesmen, suppliers, other designers, subject matter experts, and customers to create the *perfect blueprint* for a *Top Performing Business*.

He or she reviews your survey results, customer satisfaction information, and team strengths to help put together a well-balanced transformation team. The Transformation Architect is an organizer, facilitator, and workplace designer. This person works very closely with the Sponsor and Project Manager and is also a member of the Steering Committee. He/she is usually a senior Human Resources Professional or Consultant.

The Sponsor

This is a senior level management role. This person provides the resources required and is usually the business owner or a senior level executive. This individual must have clear views of the transformation objectives and business benefits. The sponsor ultimately decides the best approach if you have conflicting requirements that can't be resolved at other levels in the organization. The sponsor is responsible for ensuring other members of the management team share his or her commitment to the transformation effort. The project sponsor usually performs the final approval for changes or suggested strategies that have a global impact. The project sponsor is also on the Steering Committee and owns the budget.

The Project Manager

The Project Manager is responsible for developing the plan and collaborating with people as needed to execute the plan. This person also helps resolve issues as they arise. He or she escalates risks, high-impact problems and recommended solutions to the Steering Committee and Sponsor. A good project manager is a good communicator and has exceptional organizational skills. This individual keeps people actively engaged and continuously "plans forward" to minimize obstacles and delays. He or she will measure progress against the plan, and makes adjustments to the plan as needed while staying true to the objectives.

The Steering Committee

A senior level group that establishes the transformation objectives. They are also responsible for allocating appropriate resources, budget approval, and fostering positive support and communication throughout the organization. They meet with the Project Sponsor and Project Manager to provide direction and resolution for escalated issues. These people must act as role models for positive change. Their actions and words need to be aligned with the transformation objectives and the behaviors and attitudes that support a *Perfect Workplace*.

The Dream and Design Teams

In the upcoming chapters, you'll be asked to engage people within your organization in ways you may not have previously used. These teams can be two or ten people. It depends on the size of your organization. As you put your teams together, you'll be doing so with the intent of engaging and partnering to build a better business. Use your experts at all levels. Use the *Team Standards* in this chapter to help you put your team together.

Your Managers and Supervisors

Your managers need to be actively engaged in the transformation process because their behavior drives your results. You'll want to communicate frequently, and ask for their feedback and suggestions. You'll also want to understand their management style and ability to adapt and learn as you transform your organization. This subject is covered in depth in the *Inspire* (your managers) step of the *Motivation-at-Work* system.

Handling Resource Constraints

I'm often told, "I don't think I have the resources I need." Consider taking small steps and moving forward where you can. When you Survey, Plan, Imagine and Reflect & Design you will probably discover you have hidden talent right under your nose. Often these *Hidden Gems* have not had an opportunity to show you what they can do. Reserve judgment as you may be pleasantly surprised.

This system has designed to be scalable. In other words, the number of strategies you wish to deploy is completely in your hands based on your unique circumstances. Just follow the process; you will prioritize the strategies that are best for your organization as you go through the steps.

You will be in the best position to determine appropriate resources and what your organization can effectively handle after you've completed the first four steps—Survey, Plan, Imagine, Reflect & Design. At this point, you'll have strategies that will help you address the specific issues that are limiting your organization's potential. So, you'll have a better understanding of which strategies will have the highest impact, and the types of strengths and resources you will need as you move forward.

Team Standards

You will engage other people in your workplace transformation efforts. So you'll want to identify the people who can help you implement and manage the tasks that allow you to meet your objectives.

Paint the big picture for your team, so they can be effective. When you do this, your team understands the benefits you hope to accomplish. They also know what you expect from them, and what's most important. Your team can be far more effective when they understand how their actions impact the desired outcomes. They can help you be more effective when they know how they fit into the big picture.

Share the key strategies and processes in the *Motivation-at-Work* System with your project team, so they know where you are heading.

Use "Team Standards" to help you identify people who have exhibited behaviors that will help you achieve your objectives. Team standards also help you communicate your expectations about behaviors that are consistent with a transformation to a *Perfect Workplace*. As your project team will be responsible for implementing the transformation strategies that will take your organization to the next level, you'll want to ensure they are good role models. Their behaviors need to reflect the behaviors of the workplace you are trying to create.

Start with the *Team Standards* below. Ask for input, or have your team refine these to reflect your unique circumstances. When you finish the *Imagine* step, you will update or replace these with the *Perfect Workplace Behaviors.*

Transformation Team Members:

- □ Treat everyone with respect
- □ Are committed to quality work
- □ Strive to complete their tasks on schedule. They directly share concerns about potential delays and provide solutions to help achieve the desired project benefits as soon as possible.
- □ Actively engage the appropriate resources to define the best possible solutions
- □ Appreciate the unique talents and strengths of team members throughout the organization and ask for help and input to build commitment and enthusiasm throughout the company
- □ Embrace continuous improvement. They step out of the box even when it's not comfortable to do so.

- □ Support the best interests of the organization and can set aside their ego and personal agendas
- □ Are committed, enthusiastic and passionate about the transformation process
- □ Are excellent communicators and actively participate in defining solutions

10 Tips for Getting Results Faster

1. Build enthusiasm early by addressing a "big pain" and scheduling a "big win" early in your transformation.

2. Update your plan regularly; don't rely on memory alone.

3. Break strategies that appear "too overwhelming" into smaller pieces. That will give you a lot of little successes, which eventually lead to a GREAT BIG accomplishment.

4. Get feedback and agreement whenever possible when you establish target completion dates.

5. Don't underestimate the power of informal conversations. Ask what is working well, what's not working well, and then ask for suggested improvements. You'll learn a lot, and end up with a better plan that delivers bigger and better benefits.

6. Assign responsibility for problem-solving. Help people help you build a better business. This also builds employee engagement and commitment.

7. Manage the issues so they don't manage you. Use the *Issue Log* provided here to help you stay focused on the highest priority activities.

8. Refer back to the *10-Point Planning Checklist* if you feel your target dates spinning out of control

9. Don't let changes inadvertently alter your destination. Keep your eyes on your end results, the transformation objectives.

10. Ask questions about your objectives, vision, and goals. Then listen relentlessly so you know if your message was received as you intended. This allows you to refine your message so you can get everyone moving in the same direction. You create positive energy and reduce change resistance. This is very simple to do, yet it is extremely effective.

Other Planning Resources

If you want to learn more about project management, check out these resources.

For a software solution, templates, and free tutorials see Microsoft Project® Software Information and Templates at http://office.microsoft.com/en-us/.

Team-Based Project Management by James P. Lewis. 1998. AMACOM (The American Management Association)

T*he Project Manager's Desk Reference* by James P. Lewis 2000. McGraw-Hill, USA.

The Project Management Institute www.pmi.org. This is a membership-based organization established in 1969. They provide training and certification, and represent project management professionals in industries such as aerospace, automotive, business management, construction, engineering, financial services, information technology, pharmaceuticals, healthcare, and telecommunications. There may be a local chapter near you.

In this chapter we reviewed the planning process and why it's a critical step for success. You discovered a *10-Point Planning System* that provides a simple way for you to stay organized. The planning template will help you keep you transformation efforts on track, and you know how to diffuse the seven common areas of failure. You have tips to help you achieve results faster and a list or resources if you decide you want to know more about the art and science of project management.

You have a tool to effectively manage issues, so the issues don't manage you. The key transformation roles and team standards help you identify the skills you need to build the business of your dreams. You know that you don't have to be constrained by too few resources. The system was designed to help you move forward based on your unique needs and challenges. What is important is to move forward, one step at a time. Many small steps create major accomplishments. All you need to do is get started.

In the next step, you'll create a *Perfect Workplace* vision and get specific about the goals that will transform your vision into reality.

Chapter 5 | Step 3: Imagine Your Perfect Workplace

"First comes thought; then organization of that thought into ideas and plans; then transformation of those plans into reality. The beginning, as you will observe, is in your imagination."

~ *Napoleon Hill*

How do you create a Perfect Workplace? You start by getting crystal clear about what you want your culture to be. That is—the *behaviors, beliefs, attitudes,* and *all* other *products* of *human work and thought* associated with your business.

Your culture is the heart of your business. It is what pumps the oxygenated blood to all your vital organs. Like your heart, your culture impacts *every aspect* of your business. Your workplace culture determines the overall health of your company.

Yet, it is rare to find a business that has specific goals for creating a workplace, or a culture that supports their operational and financial goals.

Goals are created because business leaders understand the importance of having them. We know we need a target in order to continuously improve and to achieve higher levels of performance. We need goals to excel. Yet, most business leaders don't define specific goals to create a culture that will support their financial objectives. So should we be surprised when our business culture is out of alignment with our financial and operational goals? Like any living being, your culture will get sick if it's not cared for.

If you're among the few who have created specific goals for your cultural growth as well as your financial growth, congratulations! You are truly unique! If you haven't yet created a vision for your *Perfect Workplace* culture, don't feel bad, because you have a lot of company.

In this chapter, you will create a vision for your *Perfect Workplace*. Some people aren't comfortable with the word, "perfect." I say—*what other word says it better*?

A *Perfect Workplace* is *your team's joint vision* of the behaviors, beliefs, attitudes, and all other products of human work and thought that support your business's purpose (financially and otherwise).

In STEP 3: *Imagine Your Perfect Workplace;* you will:

- □ Learn how to create a clear vision of the work community you want to create
- □ Get specific about the characteristics of your *Perfect Workplace*
- □ Identify the top motivators for your organization
- □ Generate team ownership, enthusiasm, and accountability for building a better business
- □ Create effective goals that are mapped to your *Perfect Workplace Vision*
- □ Learn the difference between tasks, garbage & goals
- □ Develop a plan to identify and overcome potential obstacles

Leverage Clarity and the Natural Law of Intention

It's more important to have absolute clarity about your *Perfect Workplace* than to know how you will get there. When you have clarity about what you want to create, you'll find that the natural laws of intention line up to help you. So you start attracting opportunities that are aligned with your goals or intentions.

Brian Tracy illustrates the power of intention beautifully in a story he tells about a homing pigeon in his book *Goals! How to Get Everything You Want—Faster Than You Ever Thought Possible*. The natural law of intention works something like this. Let's say you place a homing pigeon in a covered cage and place the cage in your car. You drive one thousand miles and stop. You remove the birdcage from your car and set the pigeon free. It circles a few times and then flies home. The pigeon somehow knows or is attracted to the energy that guides him home.

People have the same natural cybernetic ability. But, *we can* also *create* attractive energy with our thoughts. If you use that attractive energy to work for you by gaining absolute clarity about what you want to create—you achieve your goals faster.

This isn't just wishful thinking; there's hard science to back it up. Scientists are only just starting to fully understand how it works. The field of quantum physics explains how our thoughts create energy and ultimately our reality.

Some of the most well-respected experts, scientists and authorities study and write about the powerful connection between thought and manifesting reality. They include luminaries such as: Lynn McTaggart , Anthony Robbins, Brian Tracy, Lynn Grabhorn, Dr. Deepak Chopra, and physicist Danah Zohar.

When you create your vision of your *Perfect Workplace,* you are putting the power of clarity and the natural law of intention to work for you.

When your vision is complete, you will use leading-edge goal setting techniques to help you create a highly motivated workplace faster.

You'll reduce the distractions, diversions and obstacles and start seeing the cultural and financial benefits faster.

What You Need to Get Started

On the following pages, you will be guided through a series of three exercises to help you:

1. Create Your *Perfect Workplace* Vision
2. Create SMART Goals that are aligned with your vision and
3. Identify and remove potential obstacles

The exercises are designed to be completed in a group brainstorming session. You will need input from a cross-chapter of folks in your organization—managers, staff, and an executive sponsor. A group that represents people in different departments and job functions will provide you with:

- ☐ A broad range of perspectives and insights
- ☐ Joint ownership and accountability for creating a better business
- ☐ Positive energy and enthusiasm

Your Perfect Workplace Design Team

Identify the people in your organization who will participate in the brainstorming session. To select your group, identify people who:

- ☐ Are committed to making your company a better place to work

- ☐ Can put their self interests aside and represent the interests of their department of group

- ☐ Have a positive, can-do attitude

- ☐ Act in ways that are aligned with the *Transformation Team Standards* outlined in Step 2

You may want to consider your informal leaders and get them involved to help build momentum and share ideas. Also consider other people in your organization that may not have been involved in the survey step.

Ask your managers and executives for recommendations when building your *Perfect Workplace Design Team.* This is the team that will help you brainstorm your vision and create your goals. So, you want a good representation across departments and job functions.

You may end up with a group of six to twelve people depending on the size of your organization. The size is not as important as having balanced representation and a group that will be able to openly share ideas without fear of being reprimanded.

Set your ground rules for brainstorming. Here are a few examples you may want to use as you create your own guiding principles.

- ☐ No criticism allowed
- ☐ Positive attitudes only
- ☐ Show mutual respect for one another
- ☐ Every idea has value
- ☐ Have fun and IMAGINE the *Perfect Workplace*

Supplies

- ☐ Whiteboard, Dry Erase Markers, and Eraser
- ☐ Pens and Paper or Legal Pads
- ☐ Easel with Flip Chart
- ☐ Permanent Market for your flip chart
- ☐ Masking tape
- ☐ A scribe to take notes
- ☐ A quiet, well-lit, comfortable conference room

Exercise 1: Create Your Vision of the Future

You start with a vision of what *can be*, what you want. Don't censure. Let your imagination create something extraordinary! We are only limited by the size of our dreams. *You can create a great workplace and achieve the financial results you want*. Don't short-change your organization in this step. There is great power in thinking BIG.

Your *Perfect Workplace Vision* will:

- ☐ **Inspire people**. *Inspire* means to *motivate*, to *fill with spirit and energy*. Inspiration is what drives ordinary people to achieve great things. It is also what is missing in many businesses.

- ☐ **Give your organization direction.** Your vision is your compass that helps your business team make decisions that are aligned with this vision. It get's everyone moving in the same direction.

- ☐ **Significantly increase your potential if you are not afraid to stretch past your comfort zone.** Go for what you and your team really want. Create something unique and spectacular. Make a difference in the lives of the people who work with you as well as your customers and vendor partners!

- ☐ **Help you prioritize and stay on track.** You'll stay focused and minimize detours and distractions. It's easy to get lost in the daily sludge of unimportant tasks that drain your energy.

- ☐ **Determine your goals.** I like to think of goals as desired outcomes that feed your spirit. They should get you and your team excited. They are the *purpose* and *intent* behind your actions. They map to more than the bottom line. They are a means of contributing your unique strengths and gifts in a way that really makes a difference in your work community and in the world around you.

- ☐ **Help you attract what you need to accomplish your goals**. When we focus on what we want, we active the *law of attraction*. The simple truth is like attracts like. So, *when we focus on what* *we want instead of what we don't want, we start drawing more positive support to us*. These are the "coincidences" that seem to come into your life right when you need them. Get clear and focus on the end result to start seeing more opportunities and gifts from the universe that will get you where you want to go faster and with greater ease.

Your vision is too important to bury in a file or desk drawer. Get it out where everyone can digest it! These are your expectations for the future, and everyone in you organization is accountable for the state of your workplace.

Empower your team to bring about a better way of doing business.

☑ Now give everyone on your Design Team some paper or a tablet. Ask the questions in this exercise and let your team write down their thoughts for a few minutes. Then go around the room and have everyone give you one item off their lists. You will create a master list on the flip chart. Your scribe will also be taking notes and will help you keep track of responses. Keep going around the room getting one idea from each person every time you circle the room. Continue to ask for feedback until you've written everything down that the brainstorming team imagined for the Perfect Workplace. As you fill up pages on your flip chart, tear them off the easel and tape them on the wall so everyone can see them. You'll need to refer to them later.

1.1 Create Your Perfect Workplace Attributes

ASK Your *Perfect Workplace* Design Team:

What are the attributes of a Perfect Workplace? What would need to happen for you to enjoy coming to work everyday? What workplace attributes would need to exist in order for you to eagerly recommend (*insert your company name*) as a great place to work? A *Perfect Workplace* means that the behaviors of all of the people in it (managers, executives, and staff) work together to achieve common goals. What does that place look like? How do the leaders act there? What are the attributes of a *Perfect Workplace*?

Here's a list to get you started. You can adopt some of the behaviors and attributes here, but let your team brainstorm and share their own thoughts.

- ☐ Management treats everyone with respect.
- ☐ Everyone is treated fairly.
- ☐ We are in the loop about what is happening in the company we work for.
- ☐ We trust each other.
- ☐ The leaders are good communicators.
- ☐ Managers listen well.
- ☐ We love working with our customers.
- ☐ We are not afraid to ask for support or help when we need it.
- ☐ Our opinions are valued.
- ☐ We feel part of a team.
- ☐ We are paid well and fairly for the work we do.
- ☐ We know what is expected of us.
- ☐ We feel like we make a difference.
- ☐ People feel pride in their work.
- ☐ There's a lot of positive energy.
- ☐ Everyone—managers, staff and executives, openly share ideas and share the credit.
- ☐ Every team member feels important.
- ☐ We know where we are going; everyone is pulling in the same direction.
- ☐ We feel great about the work we do.
- ☐ We feel comfortable asking questions and sharing our opinions.
- ☐ We are challenged every day to learn more and grow.
- ☐ Our customers love us because we do such a great job taking care of them.
- ☐ There's a lot of enthusiasm.
- ☐ The work is challenging but not overwhelming.
- ☐ We understand what we are trying to achieve as a company.
- ☐ We are trusted and share ownership in how we accomplish our departmental goals.
- ☐ People work together well as a team. There's no bickering.

- ☐ Petty gossiping is not tolerated. We care about the people we work with.
- ☐ We help each other succeed. Behavior that promotes personal interests over what is best for the team is not allowed here.
- ☐ People encourage one another to grow personally and professionally.
- ☐ The training is really good. We are given to tools and training to do our jobs well.
- ☐ This is an exciting place to work.
- ☐ We are always coming up with innovative solutions to help our customers.
- ☐ Our work quality is superior.
- ☐ We know what are customers want and are always trying to give them better products and services.
- ☐ Every team member knows how his or her work affects other departments. We know how we fit in and why our work is important.
- ☐ We have very high standards.
- ☐ We feel like we are part of a family.
- ☐ Team mates are friends, not just co-workers.
- ☐ We really like working with each other.
- ☐ We work hard, but know how to have fun too.
- ☐ Our managers are coaches; they don't "boss" or "bully" to motivate us.
- ☐ Work and personal balance is valued here.
- ☐ People show up for work when they are supposed to.
- ☐ People don't leave very often because they enjoy working here.

☑ Now remove duplicates from your master list.

These are attributes that use different wording, but have the same general intent. For example *people love working here* can be considered the same as *people like to work here*. When in doubt, always select the attribute that is the most inspiring. In this example, *people love working here* has a lot more juice. The words you choose are important, so use the words that inspire and truly motivate!

1.2 Adopt Your 10 Perfect Workplace Attributes

Ask: Refer to the master list of *Perfect Workplace* attributes we created. From that list, w*hich characteristics for your future workplace get you the most excited about working here? Which items are most important to you?*

☑ Now have everyone write down what would make it in their individual top 10 list asking the questions above.

These are the things that get people motivated and excited about coming to work!

Confirm that everyone has completed their top 10 list. Now go around the room for each item on your *master list* and ask for a show of hands to determine what is most important to the group.

Each person should vote ten times.

If you have a tie, combine two attributes if they are related, or choose a category that is not already represented on your top 10 list. (For example, Attribute 1 is—*Our managers are great coaches*, Attribute 2 is *We create the best quality widgets in the nation*). You have no other attribute about high work quality in your top ten list, but have one about teamwork and coaching, so you'd select Attribute 2.)

Our Perfect Workplace at (your company name) :

1. ______________________________

2. ______________________________

3. ______________________________

4. ______________________________

5. ______________________________

6. ______________________________

7. ____

8. ____

9. ____

10. ____

The top characteristics of a *Perfect Workplace* should include an attribute in each category to help you build a healthy, balanced culture. *Your list may look something like this one.*

Our *Perfect Workplace* at *Widget Makers Unlimited* is a business where:

1. (*Customer Service*) Our customers love us because we are always coming up with innovative solutions to their problems and we take exceptional care to give them the best possible service.

2. (*Training & Development*) Training and development is a top priority here! We are expected to grow personally and professionally, and we have plenty of opportunities for advancement.

3. (*Fair Compensation*)We are paid well and fairly for the contributions we make to the company.

4. (*Coaching*) We work closely together as a unified team. Our leaders are excellent coaches and give us the tools and support we need to do our jobs extremely well.

5. (*Commitment, Enthusiasm & Respect)* We are committed to being the best and are proud of the work we do.

6. (*Long-term Orientation*) We make decisions that consistently support long-term growth. We don't sacrifice our futures with short-term thinking.

7. (*Empowerment*) All opinions are valued, we openly share ideas and the credit for what works well and what doesn't work so well.

8. (*Employee Satisfaction*) We work hard, but know how to have fun too. We really enjoy coming to work here.

9. (*High Standards*) We have very high quality standards and accept nothing less.

10. (*Commitment, Enthusiasm & Respect)* We respect one another and communicate with honesty and integrity.

Please note the categories in parenthesis in the *TOP 10 Attribute* example were added only to show you a well-balanced list. The category description would not typically be included in your published list.

☑ Review your list now to see if it's balanced in the following categories:

- ☐ Customer Service
- ☐ Training & Development
- ☐ Fair Compensation
- ☐ Coaching
- ☐ Commitment, Enthusiasm & Respect
- ☐ Long-term Orientation
- ☐ Empowerment
- ☐ Employee Satisfaction
- ☐ High Standards

1.3 Create Your Perfect Employee Contributions

ASK: What, as an employee of a *Perfect Workplace*, will I contribute to create a *Perfect Workplace*?

You are now asking your Design Team to flip their perspective.

Another way to ask this question is: What, as an employee of a *Perfect Workplace*, do I want my customers, teammates, and manager to expect from me? Everyone on the *Design Team* should answer this, because what we individually do and say at work affects us and our teammates, customers, and business leaders.

Ultimately, the purpose of every organization is to serve their customers well. If focus is only on the bottom line(which happens all too often), then morale, motivation, and *customer satisfaction* deteriorate. The result: your customers leave and find someone that provides better service. Everyone from the CEO, to widget maker, to floor sweeper, and everyone in between, should be united about the importance of employee and customer service as they answer this question.

How people in an organization treat one another determines *employee* satisfaction, which in turn determines *customer* satisfaction.

> ☑ Give everyone two to three minutes to write down everything they can think of. Pull everything together in your master list as you did in the pervious step.

I want my customers, teammates, and manager to expect me to ….

Your list might look something like this:

- □ Show up to work on time and be ready to work when I arrive.
- □ Do the best possible work I can.
- □ Care enough about the quality of my work to ask questions if I don't understand something.
- □ Listen well.
- □ Take the time to get to know and understand my customers.
- □ Do what I can do to help create positive energy.
- □ Recognize that my attitudes and behaviors affect my workplace. I will do what I can do to make it better.
- □ Treat my co-workers and managers with respect. (*or if a manager,* Treat my co-workers and direct reports with respect.
- □ Speak only with integrity and refrain from gossiping.
- □ Be committed to doing high quality work.
- □ Work hard, but have fun too.

- ☐ Work together to support our team goals.
- ☐ Communicate with integrity.
- ☐ Be polite and positive in the words I choose.
- ☐ Help my teammates do a better job.
- ☐ Share my ideas and solutions to help build a better business.
- ☐ Strive to do what's right, even if my opinion may not be popular.
- ☐ Get to know people who work in other departments, so I can learn how my work impacts the work they do.
- ☐ Continue to actively learn so I can grow personally and professionally.
- ☐ Maintain a positive attitude.
- ☐ Refer customers to do business with my company.
- ☐ Be attentive to customer needs and provide courteous and prompt service.
- ☐ Focus on providing solutions rather than getting stuck on problems.
- ☐ Talk to my direct supervisor about concerns I have before they become issues.
- ☐ Take pride in the work I do.
- ☐ Openly and regularly share information with my team that will help us work together to achieve our department and company goals. (*If a staff member*—Ask my manager to share our departmental goals, so I can understand why my contributions are important.)

1.4 Adopt Your 10 Perfect Workplace Employee Contributions

☑ Now you'll define your Top 10 *Perfect Workplace Employee Contributions.* These are the things your Design Team believes are the greatest contributors for building a *Perfect Workplace*.

These are the things that they want to contribute and are actions that will provide the highest sense of job satisfaction and pride in their work.

> You'll use the same process you used in step 1.2. Go around the room and vote on the top items striving for balance between Customer Service, Training & Development, Fair Compensation, Coaching, Commitment, Enthusiasm & Respect, Long-term Orientation, Empowerment, Employee Satisfaction and High Standards.

Top ten contributions you would like to provide to build a better workplace

As a *(insert your company name)* **team member, I work to build a** ***Perfect Workplace*****, and to serve our customers well. I:**

1. ______________________________
2. ______________________________
3. ______________________________
4. ______________________________
5. ______________________________
6. ______________________________
7. ______________________________
8. ______________________________
9. ______________________________
10. ______________________________

Your list might look something like this:

1. (*Customer Service*) Always look for better solutions for our customers. Great customer service is my top priority!

2. (*Training & Development*) Continuously strive to grow personally and professionally so I can help my teammates, customers, and manager and have opportunities to advance my career.

3. (*Fair Compensation*) Make significant contributions to the company for which I am paid well and fairly.

4. (*Coaching*) Do what's best for the team, not what's just good for me personally.

5. (*Commitment, Enthusiasm & Respect)* Show up on time and am ready to do great work when I arrive. I am very proud or the work I do.

6. (*Long-term Orientation*) Refer people to do business with my company.

7. (*Empowerment*) Actively share my ideas for improving quality, customer service, sales, and our team culture. I proactively provide suggestions if I see things that don't support our business goals.

8. (*Employee Satisfaction*) Work hard, but also know how to have fun. I do what I can to help make this a great place to work for everyone.

9. (*High Standards*) Create and provide the highest quality products and services.

10. (*Commitment, Enthusiasm & Respect)* Respect the people I work with by choosing positive words, and communicating with honesty and integrity.

1.5 Create Your Perfect Workplace Vision Statement

☑ Now write a statement to describe your *Perfect Workplace*. Paint your picture using vivid words. Keep editing until you get it down to one or two sentences. You want your vision statement to be easy to remember so your entire team uses it. Your statement acts as a compass and helps guide decisions and actions that are in alignment with your *Perfect Workplace*.

____

____

Here are a few examples of vision statements. Strive to be succinct while catching the spirit of your most valued attributes.

- ☐ *Our business is to put people first in every way and every day. We serve our customers, partners and each other with uncompromising enthusiasm and respect.*
- ☐ *Our (your company name) team acts with the highest degree of integrity as we work together, with our vendor partners and treasured customers to help them discover their unlimited potential.*
- ☐ *We are champions of service and quality. Nobody does it better!*

The final checks

- ☐ Does your vision inspire people?
- ☐ Does it paint the picture of the top attributes and contributions as defined by your *Design Team*?
- ☐ Is it clear and easy to understand?
- ☐ Does it support your company mission statement? This might be a good time to dust it off and see if *it* supports your *Perfect Workplace* Vision.

  If your *Perfect Workplace* vision statement does not inspire, keep working on it until it does.

  Don't be afraid to think BIG—if you allow that voice of doubt inside you to say—*that won't work here*, or *it's been tried and* *didn't work,* you *will limit* your potential. Challenge people to think big and dream, *imagine—this is the stuff that keeps us motivated*!

Think about the great sports movies—*Rudy, Remember the Titans, or Hoosiers*. Do you recall how you felt after experiencing these wonderful stories? These movies endure because they inspire people. They help us see what is possible when we have a strong vision of *what can be*. When you share a strong vision with your team, you can create phenomenal energy. Get rid of small thinking and don't be afraid to think BIG.

Now you have:

1. Your Top 10 Attributes of a *Perfect Workplace*
2. The Top 10 Contributions you would like to provide to build a better workplace
3. Your vision statement

So, it's time to create the goals that will help you realize your vision of a *Perfect Workplace*.

Exercise 2: Create SMART Goals

"Goals are dreams with deadlines."
~Diana Scharf-Hunt

The power of goal setting is best illustrated by the famous study recapped in Mark McCormack's book *What They Still Don't Teach You at Harvard Business School*. In that study the 1979 MBA graduates were surveyed to see how many graduates had set goals. The question was asked—"Have you set clear, written goals for your future and made plans to accomplish them?"

The poll indicated that only 3% of the graduates had clear, written goals, and another 13% had goals but had not written them down. The remaining 84% had no goals. The authors interviewed them again ten years later in 1989 and found:

1. The 13% with *unwritten goals* were earning *twice* as much as the 84% that did not set goals.
2. However, the 3% of the graduates with *clearly written goals* were earning, on average, *10 times more* than the remaining 97% of their entire graduating class combined.[4]

These same principles apply to business teams as well as individuals.
Superior performance is tied to clarity in what you want and the laws of positive attraction that begin to work for you when you have clearly defined goals.

Be SMART

A smart goal is:

Specific—Clear-cut. For example, *we will increase customer service quality ratings* is more specific that *we will improve the quality or our service.*

Measurable—You can quantity your progress. For example; we will increase our customer service quality ratings by 15% by 10/31/2006.

Attainable—A goal should help you stretch, but it should be accomplishable given your time, resources, and other prioritized goals.

Relevant—Does this goal inspire you? Does it line up with your vision?

Time-based—Assign a date for when your goal will be accomplished.

Know the Difference: Task, Garbage, or Goal

Goals move you closer to your vision. They help you measure your progress toward your dreams. They are actions aligned with your inspiring vision. *The quality of your goals determines your future.*

Tasks are the things you need to do to keep your businesses running smoothly. Tasks are activities like paying bills, servicing equipment, and emptying trash. They are necessary, but do not lead you directly to your vision, or to what provides purpose and meaning in your business.

Garbage is stuff that you postpone or procrastinate over. They drain your energy as they hover over you waiting for you to deal with them.

Garbage and tasks don't inspire; goals do! Deal with the tasks before they become garbage so they don't drain your precious energy.

The saying that one person's garbage is another person's treasure applies here. For every thing you do not like to do, there is someone out there who loves to do it. *Do you have activities in your business that you despise, and therefore put off until they become garbage?* Consider hiring or outsourcing those activities to someone that thoroughly enjoys them. It frees you and your team up to use your strengths to contribute in ways that inspire you rather than deplete you.

To build enthusiasm and commitment: Connect your goals with your vision and purpose as you communicate your plan, tasks and employee contributions.

Your vision is your picture of what you want to accomplish. It provides clarity and paints a vivid picture of *how things will feel* and *what* your environment will look like as you achieve your goals.

Your purpose explains why; it is the "beyond the bottom line" reason you are in business. It explains why you provide the services and solutions you offer. Your purpose explains your contributions and the needs your business satisfies.

Your vision and purpose act as a giant compass. When you lose connection with your purpose and vision, your goals will begin to feel like tasks. That's when motivation declines and performance suffers.

Keep your team connected to your ever-expanding vision and a meaningful purpose and you will create an enriching, joyful work community and a top performing business.

Maintain contact with what inspired you to set your goals in the first place. Keep your vision in front of people, not just on posters, but in your communications, in job descriptions, performance appraisals, compensation plans, in your training material…you get the idea!

Develop Goals to Support Your Perfect Workplace Vision

☑ Review your Vision Statement, and Top 10 Contributions and Attributes lists with your Design Team. The intent is to identify goals that will help you create your *Perfect Workplace*. Do not be concerned yet with how you will accomplish your goals. You will do that in the *Reflect & Design* Step.

Ask : *What steps do we have to take to create this attribute or to make this contribution to create our Perfect Workplace?*

Brainstorm and list as many goals as you can. Write down your goals on a whiteboard or easel. Don't stop yet to convert to SMART goals.

Review the goals with your Design Team. Verify that it is relevant to your *Perfect Workplace* Vision and is needed to create a Top 10 attribute or contribution.

If your goal is relevant and required—convert it to a SMART Goal. Now write down the **S**pecific, **M**easurable, **A**chievable, **R**elevant and **T**ime-based actions that will help you create the *Perfect Workplace*.

1. ____

2. ____

3. ____

4. ____

5. ____
6. ____

7. ____

8. ____

9. ____

10. ____

Before moving forward, you will want to do a quick review.

Check:

- ☐ Do your goals support your business purpose?

- ☐ Do your goals follow the S.M.A.R.T formula?

- ☐ Do your goals map to your Top 10 *Perfect Workplace* Attributes and the Top 10 Perfect Employee Contributions?

- ☐ Do your goals build joint ownership for building a *Perfect Workplace*? In other words, do you have goals that involve contributions from all team members—managers, staff, executives, and vendor partners?

- ☐ Will your goals stretch your team, yet be achievable given your resources, time, and other priorities?

Exercise 3: Overcome Potential Obstacles

This step helps you identify possible issues up front. When you know the probable obstacles, you can brainstorm steps to prevent them from becoming barriers. Many change initiatives and projects fail because potential problems are not addressed in the planning and goal setting stages.

3.1 Identify Potential Problems or Obstacles

For each goal, have your team list potential barriers or obstacles that might prevent you from moving forward.

ASK: What could get in the way of achieving your goals?

Goal 1:

Goal 2:

Goal 3:

Goal 4:

Goal 5:

Goal 6:

Goal 7:

Goal 8:

Goal 9:

Goal 10:

3.2 Create Your No Roadblocks Action Plan

Now that you know what may get in your way, identify steps you can take to effectively remove these possible issues, problems or obstacles.

For each goal, have your team identify one or two things that can be done to prevent each potential obstacle from getting in your way.

ASK: *What steps can we take so these potential obstacles do NOT get in our way?*

Goal 1:

Goal 2:

Goal 3:

Goal 4:

Goal 5:

Goal 6:

Goal 7:

Goal 8:

Goal 9:

Goal 10:

When you prioritize your goals, begin with something that can give you quick success and visible benefits. Early wins create positive energy and momentum and build a foundation for ever-expanding improvements. This is a critical strategy for creating positive behavioral and cultural changes. We cover the process of prioritizing goals in more depth in Step 4—*Reflect and Design*.

In Step 3, you took big strides toward your *Perfect Workplace*. You created a clear vision of your future. Your team identified their most important *Perfect Workplace Attributes* and *Contributions*. You now have **S**pecific, **M**easurable, **A**ttainable, **R**elevant and **T**ime based goals. You also have a strategy to help you remove potential obstacles so you can achieve your goals with fewer detours.

Update your project schedule or checklist now. You'll add more details and confirm target dates when you *Reflect and Design*.

In the next step, you'll use your *Perfect Workplace* vision and goals to choose the best strategies for building a *Top Performing Team* given your unique needs.

Chapter 6 |Step 4: Reflect & Design

"We need to stop looking at work as simply a means to earning a living and start realizing it is one of the elemental ingredients of making a life."

~ *Luci Swindo*

You now have Surveys to give you a clear picture of where you stand today.

You are building your Plan to help you stay on track.

The Vision of the *Perfect Workplace* and your SMART Goals paint a clear picture of your desired outcomes.

It's time to fill in the gaps between where you are now, and where you want to go.

By filling in the gaps, you create the *Perfect Workplace* you *imagine*. You start getting the benefits as your team becomes more motivated. Your team's energy increases; your productivity, quality, and customer relationships improve, and you get a stronger culture and a healthier bottom line.

Happy, energetic, and engaged team members are close at hand.

In this chapter you will R*eview and Design* your *Perfect Workplace*.

1. You will *review* what you learned when you surveyed your employees. This step helps you gain clarity about the perceptions that drive your current business results. You need to understand the *root causes* of workplace issues and problems in order to create effective solutions. This also helps you prioritize your next steps, so you'll know where to focus first for maximum impact.

2. You will *design* by choosing the strategies that best serve your unique needs. You can use the techniques as outlined, customize them or create your own. As you design, you are mapping your goals to the specific actions that will help you create a *Perfect Workplace* and a *Top Performing* organization.

3. You will prioritize your strategies to help you get results faster.

4. You will learn specific strategies to overcome change resistance and potential obstacles that may surface.

Once you identify the gaps between where you are *today* and where you want to go *tomorrow*, you have a clear picture of your organization's gaps. You'll know what's missing in your workplace with absolute clarity.

You will start attracting ideas and opportunities to help you fill those gaps faster than you may think. Let's start with a quick review of what you've learned about your organization.

Review What You've Learned and Accomplished

Bring together everything you've learned so far.

1. **Your survey results.** *What were your biggest pains or problem areas?*

2. **Your review of performance trends**. *What patterns emerged? Which areas in your organization are struggling more than others? Why? What do the performance trends tell you about your business and workplace? Which areas are working well? Why?*

3. **Your plan to date**. This is your checklist or project schedule with your SMART goals. You'll update your plan again at the end of this step with your perfect actions and strategies.

4. **Your *Perfect Workplace* Vision Statement.** *This is your compass. It helps you stay on course. Use it to guide you to make decisions that are aligned with your objectives.*

5. **Your Top 10 List of *Perfect Workplace Attributes*.** *These are the workplace qualities most important to you and your team.* You'll be using these in some the strategies to transform your organization.

6. **Your Top 10 List of *Perfect Workplace Employee Contributions*.** *These are the most important habits you and your employees can practice to create a Perfect Workplace.* You will use these in your communication, orientation, performance evaluations, and training to create the business you want.

7. **Your SMART Goals**. *You'll need these to help you choose the strategies to achieve your goals.*

8. **Your *No Roadblocks Action Plan*.** *These are the steps you identified that will help you minimize possible obstacles.*

Now simply reflect upon what you've learned and what you've developed so far. You are grounding yourself for the next exercise so you can quickly identify the biggest challenges and your best opportunities. After you review, you are ready to select the strategies that will be most effective for your needs and goals.

This review process usually takes no more than a few hours. The time required will depend on the amount of information available and assumes you've completed each previous step.

Are you partnering with your Design Team to select the most appropriate strategies for your organization? They helped you complete the *Imagine* Step. You also want them to complete this step with you. Increase your success rate by getting your team actively involved in the transformation process.

Enlist other participants as you *implement* your *Perfect Workplace* strategies. Many of the ideas presented here encourage cross-departmental and multi-functional teams because it builds empowerment, commitment and enthusiasm. It is also a great opportunity to develop your team for future leadership opportunities.

Choose Your Strategies

"You may have the loftiest goals, the highest ideals, the noblest dreams, but remember this, nothing works unless you do."
~ Nido Qubein

Your goals and survey questions were divided into 10 key areas you need to cultivate to create a highly motivated team and a *Top Performing Business*.

The 10 Habits of Top Performing Teams

Consider the behaviors that help you create a *Perfect Workplace* and *Top Performing Business*.

Top Performing Teams are:

1. Committed and enthusiastic, and they respect one another
2. Fairly compensated for their valuable contributions
3. Led by coaches who inspire them
4. Consistently delivering superior customer service
5. Energized with high standards
6. Empowered to do their best
7. Delighted to be on your team
8. Creating high quality products and services
9. Supporting long-term growth
10. Are well trained and continuously improving their skills (*Remember it's a Journey, Not a Destination!)*

These habits probably look familiar. That's because they map directly to the S.P.I.R.I.T. survey and goal categories. This is by design.

Everything fits together to help you select strategies that map directly to your vision of a *Perfect Workplace,* AND fix the problems that limit your team's potential.

In this step, you will choose solutions that map to your goals and survey results. Bring your Design Team together to brainstorm additional ideas or modify the strategies that are presented here.

Guidelines for Choosing Your Best Strategies

Here are a few guidelines to help you choose solutions that map to your specific needs. For best results, review these guidelines before you choose your workplace improvement strategies.

- ☐ Review the entire list of strategies, tips and ideas included in this chapter.
- ☐ Select strategies that enable early successes to help you build energy and excitement. You'll see benefits faster if you choose options that fit your current resources and budget.
- ☐ Move on to bigger goals, motivational ideas and strategies as your organization grows stronger.
- ☐ Stretch enough to inspire your team, but select solutions that also match your organizational strengths. Budgets and resource availability should be considered when choosing strategies that have the highest likelihood of success.
- ☐ Implement some strategies simultaneously. Consider your resources and ability to effectively manage multiple strategies as you decide the *how, when* and *who*.
- ☐ Cover each of the Ten Key Habits needed to build Top Performing Workplace Teams. This doesn't mean you need to start with 10 different strategies. You may start with five strategies because most of the ideas presented here are designed to improve more than one area. So, you'll start seeing improvements in every category even though you may initially implement only five or six strategies.

- ☐ Select those actions, ideas or strategies that map to your vision and goals for your *Perfect Workplace*. Customize these strategies to leverage resources or programs you may already have in place. By doing this, you can get results faster.

- ☐ Use small committees or individuals to self-manage your improvement initiatives. You'll find that many of the ideas listed here encourage you to tap into the strengths of your entire team. This empowers everyone!

- ☐ Assign a project manager to track progress of the various initiatives you select to strengthen your workplace and business. This may be you, or someone else you've identified as you completed the other exercises. Look for someone who has displayed strong project management skills.

The simple things often work best, especially when you are just getting started. Keep it simple.

Perfect Workplace Strategies for Top Performing Teams

There are sixty-four strategies presented in this chapter. In addition, you'll find more ideas, tips and resources described within each of the strategies. So there are literally hundreds of ideas presented here.

You'll also find a list of the benefits, or areas that are strengthened under each individual strategy.

This design helps you choose or customize the solutions that can best address your current challenges. It helps you achieve your *Perfect Workplace* vision and goals faster because you can easily create a balanced plan that builds *top performing team habits*.
You can use these strategies, modify them, or brainstorm your own to:

- ☐ Help you resolve the root causes of less than ideal workplace motivation and . . .

□ Build your *Perfect Workplace* (*per your vision and goals*).

Here are the *Perfect Workplace* categories.

1. Build Commitment, Enthusiasm & Respect
2. Compensate Your Team Fairly For Their Valuable Contributions
3. Coach to Lead and Inspire
4. Create Superior Customer Focus
5. Energize with High Standards
6. Empower Your Entire Team
7. Delight Your Employees (*Better than employee satisfaction!*)
8. Produce Quality Products and Services
9. Promote Long-term Thinking
10. Train and Develop Your Team

Strategy 1. Keep leaders in touch. Have executives and senior managers roll up their sleeves occasionally and pitch in to serve customers. For example, Herb Kelleher, CEO of Southwest Airlines, stays in touch by helping flight attendants serve beverages. Working directly with your team and the people they serve, strengthens both employee and customer relationships. It also gives you invaluable insights into opportunities that can take your business to the next level!

This strategy builds:

1: Commitment, Enthusiasm & Respect
3: Coaching to Lead and Inspire
4: Superior Customer Focus
7: Delighted Employees

Strategy 2. Serious Suggestions. Get serious about asking for and implementing employee suggestions. If you don't actively encourage the open exchange of ideas, and then use what you learn from your team, you're closing off the stream of unlimited opportunities. Your team can provide effective, innovative solutions that save you money, improve productivity, increase customer loyalty and expand your market share. This empowering strategy builds the teamwork need for extraordinary results. Teamwork really does make the dream work!

This strategy builds:

1: Commitment, Enthusiasm & Respect
6: Team Empowerment
8: Quality Products and Services

Strategy 3. Form Creative Teams. Use cross-departmental teams to brainstorm ideas for positive cultural change, customer solutions, better processes, quality improvements, sales growth or new or improved products and services. This strategy uncovers possibilities, perspectives and insights that may otherwise go untapped. Use the processes and templates outlined in the S.P.I.R.I.T. program for added support and to get started quickly.

This strategy builds:

1: Commitment, Enthusiasm & Respect
4: Superior Customer Focus
5: High Standards
6: Team Empowerment
7: Delighted Employees
8: Quality Products and Services
9: Long-term Thinking
10: A Highly Skilled Team

Strategy 4. Provide unconventional opportunities for professional growth. Seek out enthusiastic employees to chair a committee, meeting or project. Growth doesn't always have to mean a pay raise, promotion or position change. Learning opportunities help you develop future leaders and create excitement and support for new programs and projects. Give potential leaders opportunities to create innovative processes, tools or operating guidelines. Provide opportunities for exposure to new areas, executives or areas of interest that build on individual strengths and attributes.

This strategy builds:

1: Commitment, Enthusiasm & Respect
5: High Standards
9: Long-term Thinking
10: A Highly Skilled Team

Strategy 5. Delegate more decision making authority. Allow those who are closest to a problem resolve it whenever possible. They are typically in the best position to resolve issues if they have clear guidelines and understand the scope of their authority. Policies that require excessive approvals are demoralizing and create unnecessary bottlenecks. They also discourage innovative thinking and divert manager attention from activities that can strengthen your work environment. Excessive control stifles continuous improvement and undermines leadership and employee development programs. Establish objectives and guidelines. Then allow your team to soar!

This strategy builds:

1: Commitment, Enthusiasm & Respect
4: Superior Customer Focus
6: Team Empowerment
7: Delighted Employees
8: Quality Products and Services

Strategy 6. Reward solution—oriented thinking. Encourage behaviors that shift thinking toward solutions by recognizing and rewarding behaviors that support positive and proactive solutions. Ask your team to provide viable solutions whenever they submit a problem. This simple strategy dissolves the muck and mire that creates stagnation in an organization. When you expect solutions rather than problems, you'll create a positive and empowering workplace!

This strategy builds:

2: Fair Compensation
6: Team Empowerment
8: Quality Products and Services
9: Long-term Thinking

Strategy 7. Welcome your new hires with the red carpet treatment. Give new team members a welcome card from their department members, mentor, manager or coach. Have managers provide personal introductions and schedule time to help new employees transition smoothly into their new environment. Be ready when they arrive with business cards, a clean workstation, your company goals and your *Perfect Workplace Vision & Employee Contributions*. How about flowers, balloons or lunch with their mentor or manager? When was the last time you were delighted by a simple act of kindness? Imagine the loyalty and positive energy you can create with a little red carpet treatment!

This strategy builds:

1: Commitment, Enthusiasm & Respect
7: Delighted Employees
10: A Highly Skilled Team

Strategy 8. Celebrate successes to close your fiscal year on a positive note. Close your year with a review of accomplishments and opportunities for growth. This provides positive momentum and a foundation for a high-energy launch into your new year. Encourage active participation and joint ownership for creating success throughout your entire organization. Have employees and managers define their goals based on your objectives for the upcoming year. Hand out performance awards and recognition certificates to teams or individuals that met or exceeded goals. This is a perfect time to reconnect with powerful messages that support meaningful work!

This strategy builds:

1: Commitment, Enthusiasm & Respect

2: Fair Compensation
5: High Standards
9: Long-term Thinking

Strategy 9. Implement an *enlightened leader* development program. Assign experienced managers who embody the enlightened leadership principles as mentors. Refer to step five for more information about the enlightened leader principles, then create a recommended reading list that supports those attributes. You can use the recommended resources in this book as a guide. You do not have to spend a lot of money on leadership development in order to have a top notch team. However, you do need to provide focus and encouragement to develop the type of leadership that creates *top performance* and a *perfect workplace*.

This strategy builds:

1: Commitment, Enthusiasm & Respect
3: Coaching to Lead and Inspire
4: Superior Customer Focus
6: Team Empowerment
7: Delighted Employees
9: Long-term Thinking
10: A Highly Skilled Team

Strategy 10. Slay sacred cows. Organizations get entrenched in the "way we've always done it" thinking. Have your managers and employees give away fun trophies, such as a cow bell or Holstein figurine, every time they discover someone that is stepping out of the box with innovative thinking that improves a process, builds stronger customer relationships or opens the door to new business opportunities!

This strategy builds:

1: Commitment, Enthusiasm & Respect
3: Coaching to Lead and Inspire
4: Superior Customer Focus
5: High Standards
6: Team Empowerment

7: Delighted Employees
8: Quality Products and Services
9: Long-term Thinking
10: A Highly Skilled Team

Strategy 11. Use symbolism to support positive changes. Symbols are an effective way to communicate and emphasize key points. They enhance the impact of text and can simplify complex concepts. For example, you might attach a dinosaur to an outdated process or system to create a shift in thinking that frees your team for change and growth. Symbols can be used in a fun way to remind your team about the habits, attitudes, and actions needed to create a *Perfect Workplace* and a *Top Performing* organization!

This strategy builds:

1: Commitment, Enthusiasm & Respect
4: Superior Customer Focus
5: High Standards
6: Team Empowerment
7: Delighted Employees
8: Quality Products and Services
9: Long-term Thinking

Strategy 12. Give permission to make mistakes along with the accountability for resolving them when they do occur. This strategy is a scary notion for some people. However, it's impossible to create a dynamic, enthusiastic and innovative business if people work in constant fear of making a mistake. With the appropriate guidelines, you can minimize risks while creating a positive shift in your culture and business. This strategy encourages people to continuously expand and improve. It also can be used to foster teamwork as employees work together to develop ideas, improve processes and resolve issues.

This strategy builds:

1: Commitment, Enthusiasm & Respect
2: Fair Compensation

6: Team Empowerment
7: Delighted Employees
8: Quality Products and Services
9: Long-term Thinking
10: A Highly Skilled Team

Strategy 13. Energize your meetings. Are your meetings inspiring and productive? Do they follow a formal agenda and start and end on time? Do people arrive prepared? Are action items and responsibilities clearly outlined prior to meeting adjournment? To zap unproductive meetings, use a timer, assign a team member to keep a meeting on track, and use props or visuals to make important points. *The key here is to eliminate unproductive, unnecessary and ineffective meetings.* They drain everyone's energy and enthusiasm. There is a valid reason why the phrase "death by meeting" is circulating in corporate America. Then when you do need to meet, set clear objectives in advance and use an agenda. Give people some much needed time back in their schedules and watch your productivity soar!

This strategy builds:

1: Commitment, Enthusiasm & Respect
3: Coaching to Lead and Inspire
5: High Standards

Strategy 14. Promote team suggestions. Implement a suggestion program that rewards an *entire department* or *team* for suggestions that solve a customer or company problem. This strategy encourages teamwork and builds a sense of community because it provides an opportunity for employees to build stronger relationships. Your team also receives the added bonuses of enthusiasm, pride and commitment that naturally expand when we share credit for our successes.

This strategy builds:

1: Commitment, Enthusiasm & Respect

3: Coaching to Lead and Inspire
4: Superior Customer Focus
6: Team Empowerment
8: Quality Products and Services
10: A Highly Skilled Team

Strategy 15. Thank your employees with pancakes. Have managers cook and serve breakfast or lunch for employees once a month or quarter. You could also make this an employee recognition event or discuss important news, anniversaries or birthdays. This activity is a simple, yet powerful way for your managers to thank their team for their valuable contributions.

This strategy builds:

1: Commitment, Enthusiasm & Respect
3: Coaching to Lead and Inspire
7: Delighted Employees

Strategy 16. Minimize the filters. Get your important messages out faster by reducing the filtering systems as much as possible. As messages are relayed through multiple managers and supervisors, sometimes the key points get lost or misinterpreted. Think of the game telephone and how the message at the end of the chain was quite different than the original message. Use weekly or monthly President or CEO meetings with your entire staff to discuss important goals, progress and initiatives. This provides employees, at all levels, with an opportunity to receive one message and feel connected to the big picture. This strategy also helps your senior leaders stay in touch, which strengthens trust and partnerships across the organization.
This strategy builds:

1: Commitment, Enthusiasm & Respect
3: Coaching to Lead and Inspire
4: Superior Customer Focus
5: High Standards
7: Delighted Employees

9: Long-term Thinking
10: A Highly Skilled Team

Strategy 17. Start a high octane company newsletter. I know; you've heard the newsletter strategy before. That may be true, but consider the degree to which most company newsletters are actually tied to business *objectives.* Most newsletters are simply not effective because they don't have a clear reason for being. So, they usually end up listing employee anniversary dates, birthdays and new hire information. This news is certainly important, but it falls short of maximizing this tool's full potential. Now consider how you might use a newsletter to educate your team, build enthusiasm and a sense of purpose. How about creating positive energy and support for a new program or initiative? You can share industry news so your team learns more about emerging trends and customer preferences. You can recognize departments and team members for their accomplishments. You can include inspiring stories or quotes that lift your team to new heights. Your newsletter can be published and distributed electronically via email or intranet, or you can use the traditional paper method. A company newsletter can be a great training tool and change agent. It can promote the "what's in it for me?" benefits that motivate your team to improve customer service, product quality or your business processes. You can use the power of words to build a sense of community to improve employee retention. A newsletter can tear down walls and reduce the interdepartmental turf wars that sometimes surface in larger organizations. This strategy can be one of your best investments if tied to your business and P*erfect Workplace* objectives. It does require time, resources and planning. If done well, a company newsletter can be the center piece of an effective communication strategy that inspires and drives positive and lasting change.

This strategy builds:

1: Commitment, Enthusiasm & Respect
4: Superior Customer Focus
5: High Standards
9: Long-term Thinking
10: A Highly Skilled Team

Strategy 18. Promote MBWA. *Management By Walking Around* stimulates one—on—one communication. Set expectations that managers need plenty of floor time so they can connect with the people that report to them. Managers have more influence on employee retention that any other single factor. How they are perceived matters. Do your managers listen well? Are they trusted? Are they seen as a good coach? Do your managers know what their team needs to do their jobs well? Are they responsive to the needs of their team? We can not build leadership skills or improve cultural health if we're behind a desk all day. Leaders get disconnected when they spend too much time in meetings and in their offices. Observe and reward your managers for building stronger relationships with their teams.

This strategy builds:

1: Commitment, Enthusiasm & Respect
3: Coaching to Lead and Inspire
5: High Standards
6: Team Empowerment
7: Delighted Employees
8: Quality Products and Services
10: A Highly Skilled Team

Strategy 19. Get involved in your community. No business is an island. The people within your organization make decisions and take actions that directly impact the community in which you operate. Whether you are global or local, you have an opportunity to contribute something truly special that leaves your world better than you found it. Find a local charity or cause that is aligned with your values, products or services. Let your managers and staff select or vote on a program or project that has real meaning to them. Then give them time to get involved. This deepens commitment and helps people connect with a greater purpose. It's important to give back to the communities in which we serve. It feels good and helps us attract like minded customers and employees!

This strategy builds:

1: Commitment, Enthusiasm & Respect
4: Superior Customer Focus

6: Team Empowerment
9: Long-term Thinking
10: A Highly Skilled Team

Strategy 20. Start a Refer—a—friend program. When you build a sense of community and belonging, you build employee commitment and loyalty. People naturally want to feel they are part of a community that accepts and appreciates them. This philosophy can help you find, hire and retain talented team members that are the best fit for your organization. Pair this strategy with your *Perfect Workplace Attributes* to attract and hire employees that value the types of behaviors you want to expand throughout your business. To increase participation in the program, you may want to consider offering a referral bonus or extra vacation time when an employee refers a new hire. Many organizations distribute an incentive when a referral becomes an employee and remains on their team for specified time period. Typically, higher incentives require longer retention requirements. Some companies will distribute 50% of a bonus when a referred employee begins work and then distribute the balance when the new employee finishes training or reaches a specific milestone. Of course, always check with a qualified professional to determine applicable tax laws, regulations and requirements.

This strategy builds:

1: Commitment, Enthusiasm & Respect
2: Fair Compensation
9: Long-term Thinking

Strategy 21. Help your employees attract more of your *perfect* customers. Do your employees *know* your perfect customer? Do they know their attributes and characteristics? Do they understand what makes your perfect customers tick and what they want and need? If not, put this on your "must do list". Your employees can't adequately service your customers, let alone refer them to your company, if they don't know what your perfect customer looks like. So start by introducing your team to your perfect customer. Then give your team the tools they need to help you build your business.

Consider distributing business *referral* cards your employees can give to people when they're asked do you know anyone who ... provides your specific product or service? You can design cards with a "Referred by" space so employees can write in their name and you can track the source of the referral. You can tie referrals to a bonus or recognition program for an added lift.

Add a special customer discount or promotion that's good with employee referrals only. There are literally hundreds of things you could do to help your employees help you attract more and better customers. Just make it fun and light and don't expect people to use aggressive tactics. A hard sell approach will backfire if people feel they are being asked to do something that is not aligned with their value system. People naturally want to help other people solve problems. That is what you do when you provide a referral, you're helping someone solve a problem or fulfill a need. So, if you approach this strategy with the idea that you'll give your employees the tools they need to help your perfect customers find you, you'll be on a very "attractive" track. Know what your employees value. Then show your gratitude by giving your team what they value most.

If you'd like more help defining your perfect customer, see www.perfectcustomer.com to download an affordable and very effective and enlightening marketing planner. This is a simple, yet powerful tool that helps you attract more of your perfect customers.

This strategy builds:

1: Commitment, Enthusiasm & Respect
2: Fair Compensation
4: Superior Customer Focus
7: Delighted Employees
9: Long-term Thinking

Strategy 22. Get the word out. Provide everyone with a framed copy of your *Perfect Workplace Vision Statement* and *Contributions*. Creating a shift in thinking and ultimately in your workplace requires conscious and consistent communication that is aligned with your unique objectives. Not just once, but repeatedly in different formats, venues and styles. Use a design that's inspiring and pleasing to the eye so people want to look at it everyday. Consider using a contest to engage your team in designing themes that lift your spirit and support your vision and contribution statements. Add graphics and pictures to strengthen your message. Give people a reason to proudly display positive and powerful words on their desk or in their work area. Use the power of positive words to feed your spirit and your bottom line!

This strategy builds:

1: Commitment, Enthusiasm & Respect
3: Coaching to Lead and Inspire
4: Superior Customer Focus
5: High Standards
8: Quality Products and Services
9: Long-term Thinking
10: A Highly Skilled Team

Strategy 23. Get everyone moving in the same direction. Add your *Perfect Workplace Vision, Goals* and *Employee Contributions* to your company Intranet Site and Orientation handbook. Think about where your employees go for information and where they gather to eat lunch, take breaks, work and relax. Then go there with your message. The key to getting everyone moving in the same direction is conscious and consistent communication. Make it fun, inspiring and light. You probably have resources on your team who could help you come up with other creative ways to get the word out. Think about letters from the president, bulletin boards, pens or mugs with catchy and inspiring phrases, affirming quotes on your intranet site, updates about special projects and initiatives, newsletters, "Tickets to Success" updates delivered to you employee's inboxes and the list goes on. Start with the tools and resources you already have in place to get you started quickly. You can add other tools when you're ready to do so.

If you're looking for messages that are filled with wisdom, insight and inspiration see Ralph Marston's *Daily Motivator* at www.greatday.com. I've bee a subscriber for years and look forward to reading it every day. These brief yet compelling and effective insights are delivered six days per week to your inbox. This is an affordable tool that can enrich your personal and professional life. I hope you find it as inspiring as I have.

This strategy builds:

1: Commitment, Enthusiasm & Respect
3: Coaching to Lead and Inspire
5: High Standards
7: Delighted Employees
8: Quality Products and Services
9: Long-term Thinking
10: A Highly Skilled Team

Strategy 24. Get the right people on the bus. Tie your *Perfect Workplace Contributions* into your hiring, screening, and succession planning processes. You know the qualities and attributes that support your unique objectives. Now you can create questions to help you and your hiring managers identify the candidates who are the best fit given your *Perfect Workplace Attributes*. Use the insights you've gained through the S.P.I.R.I.T. process to expand purpose, passion and profits in your organization. You now have the tools to help you create something extraordinary. Ask yourself where you can use these tools and insights to help you create fulfilling and meaningful work and a top performing business.

This strategy builds:

1: Commitment, Enthusiasm & Respect
4: Superior Customer Focus
5: High Standards
8: Quality Products and Services
9: Long-term Thinking
10: A Highly Skilled Team

Strategy 25. Examine your employee performance review process. Do you recognize and reward your managers and staff for contributing to both cultural AND financial growth? You can't maintain steady financial growth year over year unless you have the right foundation. A key component in that foundation is the environment that supports your specific goals, hopes and dreams. So, be certain that your performance evaluation process recognizes people who lift up your organization by being problem solvers and agents for positive change. These are the individuals who strengthen your work environment by actively supporting your *Perfect Workplace Attributes*. They are creating and building the foundation you need to succeed. You will expand and grow in direct proportion to your ability to effectively recognize and reward those behaviors that embody your vision of a *Perfect Workplace.*

This strategy builds:

1: Commitment, Enthusiasm & Respect
2: Fair Compensation
3: Coaching to Lead and Inspire
4: Superior Customer Focus
5: High Standards
7: Delighted Employees
8: Quality Products and Services
10: A Highly Skilled Team

Strategy 26. If it matters, measure it. Develop your own version of a *Balanced Perfect Workplace Scorecard* and use it for coaching, training, determining compensation and evaluating performance. Measure and monitor financial AND cultural trends by company, division, manager and employee to get a snapshot of how employees, departments and managers are performing compared to others or a prior time period. Incorporate the trends that are meaningful to your organization given your specific objectives. Common performance indicators for measuring growth and overall health include: net profit changes, customer retention rates, customer satisfaction ratings, quality or defect rates, sales rates, employee turnover, absenteeism, productivity/output changes, and employee survey and satisfaction ratings. Start with the data that is readily available, then add and refine elements as your needs change. Don't get bogged down in the details, but do have a means to measure what's important. That's the only way you can truly determine your long term progress.

This strategy builds:

1: Commitment, Enthusiasm & Respect
2: Fair Compensation
3: Coaching to Lead and Inspire
4: Superior Customer Focus
5: High Standards
6: Team Empowerment
7: Delighted Employees
8: Quality Products and Services
9: Long-term Thinking
10: A Highly Skilled Team

Strategy 27. Give them the facts. Tell your employees and vendors regularly what your customers think about your products and services. Share the positive and the not so positive trends, letters and comments. Invite feedback and solutions. When we share information, we create partnerships that help us expand our ability to conceptualize what's possible. Both employees and suppliers have unique perspectives that can provide insights and open doors to solutions and opportunities for growth. When we share information with our suppliers, we help them learn more about their market so they too can be more responsive and grow with their customers. When we share information with our employees, we help them connect with meaningful work. Good information enables employees to provide *perfectly aligned service*. It also allows them to share ideas and generate innovative solutions that can help them, their coworkers, you, your customers and your suppliers.

This strategy builds:

4: Superior Customer Focus
6: Team Empowerment
8: Quality Products and Services
9: Long-term Thinking
10: A Highly Skilled Team

Strategy 28. Assign a team to review your policies and procedures for alignment with empowering practices. Do your policies and procedures empower your team or treat them like children? Policies and practices that overburden your organization with excessive approvals are demoralizing and do not build the leaders around you. Examine your policies, practices and procedures and make changes to ensure they build trust and joint accountability for your organization's success. Provide guidelines, but don't micromanage. It kills innovative thinking, employee engagement, enthusiasm, and empowerment.

If you are looking for tools to help you manage your important documents or automate and streamline business processes, you may want to check out www.transparentlogic.com. They provide cost effective software solutions that are intuitive and graphical, so your business team can actually define and refine your processes and procedures quickly. So you can be more responsive to your customers. Their tools also help you implement employee process improvement suggestions faster and with fewer risks.

This strategy builds:

1: Commitment, Enthusiasm & Respect
4: Superior Customer Focus
6: Team Empowerment
7: Delighted Employees
8: Quality Products and Services
9: Long-term Thinking

Strategy 29. Create a peer recognition program. If you want to build enthusiasm and empower your team, provide an opportunity for team members to honor peers who actively support your *Perfect Workplace Habits*. It's especially rewarding to be recognized by coworkers when you go above and beyond the call of duty. Narrow your program to strengthen a specific area such as customer service if you want to simplify the program. By concentrating your focus, you can amplify your results in an area that has the potential for the greatest growth or return.

This strategy builds:

1: Commitment, Enthusiasm & Respect
2: Fair Compensation
5: High Standards
6: Team Empowerment
7: Delighted Employees

Strategy 30. Use ongoing employee satisfaction (*delight*) surveys. Consider doing surveys twice yearly initially and then move to an annual schedule once you've achieved your initial goals or a specific milestone. This strategy gives you the ability to monitor the health of your company and anticipate potential issues before they become major hurdles. You gain valuable insights about the beliefs that drive your financial results. We become what we think, so it's important to understand what we are creating through our attitudes and thoughts. A regular survey helps you measure your progress and choose the best strategies so you achieve your goals faster and with greater ease. Surveys also tell your team that their opinion is important. What they say matters and you value their input. The goodwill you can generate with this tool is priceless. Add that to the inherent benefits of aligning your strategies with the wisdom gained and you are on a solid path to an extraordinary business!

This strategy builds:

1: Commitment, Enthusiasm & Respect
4: Superior Customer Focus
8: Quality Products and Services
9: Long-term Thinking

Strategy 31. Adopt a philosophy of continuous improvement. Keep raising your performance bar higher, both culturally and financially. Create annual goals that help you build the quality of your work environment as well as your customer service, productivity, product quality and financial performance. Involve team members across job functions, department and locations to build enthusiasm and joint ownership. Don't forget to celebrate your successes. It's important to pause every now and then to enjoy the journey. Together we really are better!

This strategy builds:

1: Commitment, Enthusiasm & Respect
4: Superior Customer Focus
5: High Standards
6: Team Empowerment
7: Delighted Employees
8: Quality Products and Services
9: Long-term Thinking

Strategy 32. Inspire your team. Consider a motivational speaker to help you give your team a quick lift. Everyone needs a little booster shot occasionally. Your organization benefits because a good speaker can bring new perspectives that open doors to new opportunities. Check out Debbie Allen, an international business expert and top motivational speaker at www.debbieallen.com. Also see the National Speakers Association at www.nsaspeaker.org, do a Google search for local resources or ask an associate for a referral. This is not a stand alone solution, but is a great supplement to a perfect workplace initiative. It creates excitement and energy and communicates that you're committed to taking your team to the next level!

This strategy builds:

1: Commitment, Enthusiasm & Respect
3: Coaching to Lead and Inspire
10: A Highly Skilled Team

Strategy 33. Empower your managers to recognize employee behaviors that build great customer relationships with "on the spot" rewards. The intent here is to instantly show gratitude for actions that support your goals and objectives. Gestures of appreciation don't have to be expensive to be effective. You can use thank you notes, movie tickets, certificates, trophies, pins, extra vacation time, gift certificates to restaurants or scratch & win game tickets as incentives. Appreciation is contagious and the positive energy spreads quickly. The intent is not to create an environment in which people expect to be continuously rewarded. The philosophy is to genuinely show gratitude for a job well done. Everyone wants to feel appreciated. Show appreciation and you'll naturally receive more of what you desire in your personal and professional experiences

This strategy builds:

1: Commitment, Enthusiasm & Respect
3: Coaching to Lead and Inspire
4: Superior Customer Focus
5: High Standards
7: Delighted Employees
10: A Highly Skilled Team

Strategy 34. Send personal thank you notes from the company president. This gesture can have tremendous impact when done consistently to recognize individuals who go above and beyond the call of duty. Imagine receiving a handwritten note or letter that says thank you for your valuable contributions. Your extra efforts are recognized and appreciated and you are important! This message is beyond powerful when done with sincerity. Appreciation is an essential ingredient for enabling your organization to shine as brightly as it can.

This strategy builds:

1: Commitment, Enthusiasm & Respect
3: Coaching to Lead and Inspire
7: Delighted Employees
8: Quality Products and Services
9: Long-term Thinking

Strategy 35. Host a cross—departmental barbeque for fun, networking and problem solving. Who says you can't have fun while you're solving problems, improving communication, or streamlining a process? Mix and match employees from different departments at tables and give them a problem to solve along with some tasty food. Discuss the solutions after you've provided time for brainstorming. Reserve judgment and have some fun getting people to step out of the box. Give out certificates to recognize participation or innovative solutions. This experience helps tear down communication barriers between departments and builds employee commitment and teamwork. Don't forget to send follow up communication to let your team know how their input benefits everyone.

This strategy builds:

1: Commitment, Enthusiasm & Respect
4: Superior Customer Focus
6: Team Empowerment
7: Delighted Employees
8: Quality Products and Services
9: Long-term Thinking
10: A Highly Skilled Team

Strategy 36. Design and display an *Accountability Roadmap*. This is a visual tool that helps everyone in your company understand "who does what". To be effective, make your roadmap fun and easy to follow. When you know how your work fits into the big picture, you can understand why your work is important. The big picture helps us connect with meaningful and fulfilling work. Post your roadmap in a high traffic area so people can easily refer to it on a regular basis. Understanding the next steps in a process helps everyone appreciate how their work impacts your customers, their coworkers and other processes. This strategy opens up the possibilities for creative thinking and builds bridges across your organization.

This strategy builds:

1: Commitment, Enthusiasm & Respect

6: Team Empowerment
8: Quality Products and Services
10: A Highly Skilled Team

Strategy 37. Celebrate diversity. Post employee stories about favorite family recipes, where they grew up or went to school, favorite hobbies, school mascots, and their most treasured holiday memories and traditions. When we connect with one another in meaningful ways, we tear down the barriers that separate us and make us feel small. This simple activity helps people value one another's unique qualities and experiences, while building appreciation for the things that also connect us. When we see one another with new eyes, amazing things happen!

This strategy builds:

1: Commitment, Enthusiasm & Respect
7: Delighted Employees

Strategy 38. Help your employees and leaders connect and have some fun. Post baby pictures of your managers and leaders on a company intranet site or bulletin boards. Have a contest to see how many people can guess each baby's identity. Who doesn't smile when they see a baby picture? Spread some joy and positive buzz and help your team see one another in a new way
This strategy builds:

1: Commitment, Enthusiasm & Respect
7: Delighted Employees

Strategy 39. Ensure your compensation and review process is equitable and tied to cultural, customer, financial, and quality contributions. Confirm that your managers can and do explain how your compensation system works to their direct reports. This is simple, but often overlooked as we get caught up in our daily routines. If your compensation system is perceived as unfair, too complex or unaligned with your important objectives, it is ineffective. Take the time to get this one right. Review the opinions from your employee surveys to see what your team believes about your compensation and evaluation processes. Use a task force to come up with creative ideas and solutions. Map compensation to your cultural and financial goals as well as to the things your employees value most

This strategy builds:

1: Commitment, Enthusiasm & Respect
2: Fair Compensation
3: Coaching to Lead and Inspire
4: Superior Customer Focus
5: High Standards
8: Quality Products and Services
9: Long-term Thinking

Strategy 40. Establish guidelines that tie recognition and rewards to your most important financial and cultural goals. To promote real financial growth recognize, reward and compensate based on *profitable* sales, not just top-line revenue. For stellar cultural growth, such as encouraging dynamic problem-solving, reward people who proactively resolve problems, not those who just minimize them. For customer service—reward people for building customer loyalty, not those who just have a low number of complaints. Examine your focus. Do your practices encourage your team to shoot for the stars or do they merely support mediocre performance?
This strategy builds:

1: Commitment, Enthusiasm & Respect
4: Superior Customer Focus
5: High Standards
7: Delighted Employees
8: Quality Products and Services
9: Long-term Thinking

Strategy 41. Market your success. Build and use a continuous communication strategy to expand momentum and positive energy in and around your business. Maximize exposure for individual and team contributions that support your goals and objectives. Shout from the rooftop when you launch a new program, achieve important goals, give an award for exemplary performance, attract more ideal customers or make progress on major initiatives. Use the power of positive progress to keep you moving in the direction of unlimited potential and endless opportunities!

This strategy builds:

1: Commitment, Enthusiasm & Respect
3: Coaching to Lead and Inspire
10: A Highly Skilled Team

Strategy 42. Zap the "us versus them" thinking. There lies within many people an unconscious need to be right and make others wrong, so they can feel better about themselves. This type of thinking is easy to adopt because it feeds our ego. But, it also destroys happiness and the joy that comes when we collaborate with one another. Working together to celebrate our unique gifts and contributions allows us to grow and move to the next level personally and professionally. Together we accomplish far more than we can alone. Whenever possible bring people together to help them connect in meaningful ways. Adopt a zero tolerance policy for behaviors that tear down morale. Use companywide update meetings to encourage networking across departments and organizational levels. Ask for volunteers to conduct departmental tours to build understanding and respect across your organization. Schedule time for new hires and established employees to tour every department so they can get to know other people and learn more about what they do. Have your leaders walk around and interact with people in various job functions on a regular basis. Ask for input and get to know people. Use your newsletters or intranet site to highlight individual contributions in every department and functional role. There is tremendous potential in all of us just waiting to be tapped. Use the techniques outlined here to build an extraordinary community and business.

This strategy builds:

1: Commitment, Enthusiasm & Respect
3: Coaching to Lead and Inspire
6: Team Empowerment

7: Delighted Employees
9: Long-term Thinking

Strategy 43. Step away from your inbox. How much time do you spend weeding through your email every day? Does every email you read add value or does it distract you from doing something more meaningful? What are you missing when you are entrenched in your inbox? Our addiction to electronic communication can devour precious energy, delay important decisions and create misunderstandings and roadblocks. Companies become depersonalized when they rely on email as their primary communication tool. Coach your managers and employees to walk to someone's office, or pick up the phone to engage in person—to—person communication as frequently as possible. Many communication issues and "email wars" are caused by the limitations of this particular communication tool. It is only one tool and was never designed to replace every form of human communication. Use email with care and when documentation is important. The need for human interaction and social contact is a basic human need which can't be replaced by electronic media alone

This strategy builds:

2: Fair Compensation
4: Superior Customer Focus
10: A Highly Skilled Team

Strategy 44. Challenge your managers and executives to learn a new leadership skill every month or quarter. Tie ongoing learning to leader compensation. Many issues occur because employees get promoted to management positions based on their productivity or task experience, not their ability to guide, coach and mentor. Many organizations promote people into managerial roles, and then provide no tools or incentives for developing sound leadership skills. This practice can fill and organization with managers who simply do not have an aptitude or interest in developing people. Should it be a surprise then when the "dream team" doesn't materialize? Stop the insanity now. Set solid management selection criteria mapped to your *Perfect Workplace* goals and the E*nlightened Leadership* behaviors that support your goals. Refer to step five for more information about the enlightened leader behaviors. Then give your leaders tools and encourage them to continuously expand their ability to conceptualize what's possible. *Now that's inspiring!*

This strategy builds:

1: Commitment, Enthusiasm & Respect
3: Coaching to Lead and Inspire
5: High Standards
6: Team Empowerment
10: A Highly Skilled Team

Strategy 45. Reward *Enlightened Leadership* behaviors. Are you supporting your goals by rewarding leadership habits that are tied to your *Perfect Workplace* goals? Every manager should review cultural and financial performance trends with their direct reports on a regular basis. Energy flows where attention goes! Focused attention is required for lasting change. Compare performance trends across departments so you know who is leading in a manner that supports your cultural and financial objectives and who might need some help.

This strategy builds:

1: Commitment, Enthusiasm & Respect
3: Coaching to Lead and Inspire
4: Superior Customer Focus
5: High Standards
9: Long-term Thinking
10: A Highly Skilled Team

Strategy 46. Use low-cost learning techniques to support your goals. Give away magazine or online subscriptions to new managers and employees. Develop a recommended reading list. Distribute books or online articles. Encourage everyone to learn and grow throughout your organization for their own benefit as well as your business. When we grow, it positively impacts every area of our lives. When we learn a new professional skill, we can often apply what we've learned to improve our personal lives as well. When we grow personally, our professional performance also improves. Despite our attempts to compartmentalize our lives into separate little containers, we live a delicate balance of diverse roles, aspirations, hope, dreams and priorities. We benefit and those around us benefit when we learn new skills for our own evolution and well being

This strategy builds:

3: Coaching to Lead and Inspire
7: Delighted Employees
9: Long-term Thinking
10: A Highly Skilled Team

Strategy 47. Use *Perfect Workplace* banners and screensavers to recognize those who volunteer to serve on a committee. Give away workstation banners, pins, pens, t—shirts or motivational prints. Keep the inspiring messages flowing and you will see a positive and lasting difference in your environment and on your personal and professional bottom line.

This strategy builds:

1: Commitment, Enthusiasm & Respect
7: Delighted Employees

Strategy 48. Shed light on the reality of change. Mountains of books have been written about change management. Although the methodology is helpful; these books are usually more complicated than they need to be. Here is a basic fact of life—if we are not evolving or growing, we are dying. It's that simple. The angst that comes with change is almost always due to fear of the unknown. We fear the unknown is worse than our current situation. The reality—when we grow, we expand our comfort zones. What was once uncomfortable is now quite comfortable. Reset the limiting belief that says change is the exception. It isn't, it's the rule. The universe is continually expanding and so too are we. It is our resistance to change that creates our pain and suffering. Organizational inertia is the kiss of death for any business. Educate and show compassion in your communication about changes in your organization. Build trust with open communication and dialogue. Shed light on the unknown. Help your team expand their ability to conceptualize what's possible. Then, trust in basic human goodness.

This strategy builds:

1: Commitment, Enthusiasm & Respect
5: High Standards
6: Team Empowerment
7: Delighted Employees
8: Quality Products and Services
10: A Highly Skilled Team

Strategy 49. Purge the perks that create divisiveness. Many companies unknowingly create barriers when they use perks for managers and executives only. Common practices like reserved parking for executives, and separate break rooms by department or job function can create communication barriers, destroy morale and discourage innovative thinking. These practices can unconsciously communicate "we think we're better or more important than you are". Obviously this is not a message that builds team spirit. Consider instead reserved parking spots for top performance or exemplary customer service. What is better for your business — collaboration and unbridled enthusiasm or outmoded practices that support class consciousness?

This strategy builds:

1: Commitment, Enthusiasm & Respect
3: Coaching to Lead and Inspire
6: Team Empowerment
7: Delighted Employees

Strategy 50. Give *special project clearance* to create excitement and encourage involvement in new projects. Build awareness and recognize engaged team members with t—shirts, certificates, "honorary degrees" or lunches with leaders. Fun is not a four letter word and is, in fact, a major driver of longevity and low turnover. Make special projects fun and enjoyable and you won't have a shortage of volunteers. When people get involved they forge deeper relationships with coworkers and develop skills they can use at work and in other areas of their lives. Don't be afraid of a little humor to get energized!

1: Commitment, Enthusiasm & Respect
4: Superior Customer Focus
6: Team Empowerment
7: Delighted Employees
9: Long-term Thinking

Strategy 51. Form a pay-plan committee. Tell your team they can design their own compensation plan and if reasonable, it will be approved. Provide your cultural and financial goals as guidelines. You may be pleasantly surprised by the creativity and innovative ideas that surface. You'll also gain insights into what your team values most. It isn't always about the money. Often people value progressive policies that support balance, quality of life, autonomy and flexibility more than pure compensation. Build trust, enthusiasm and commitment by creating compensation plans that truly empower and enrich your team and your bottom line!

This strategy builds:

1: Commitment, Enthusiasm & Respect
2: Fair Compensation
6: Team Empowerment
8: Quality Products and Services
10: A Highly Skilled Team

Strategy 52. **Consider 360 reviews or a hybrid approach**. You can use a 360 review process (using peers, supervisor, direct reports and customer feedback) or a similar philosophy for every employee in your company, not just managers and executives. Peer reviews can be a very powerful way to create positive changes that build better businesses. Compensate based on a balanced review process that includes qualitative and quantitative measures and financial and cultural contributions. Of course, create guidelines that support constructive feedback and honor the integrity and privacy of everyone involved. Always check with a qualified Human Resources professional and attorney to ensure you are compliant before launching a new program.

This strategy builds:

1: Commitment, Enthusiasm & Respect
2: Fair Compensation
4: Superior Customer Focus
6: Team Empowerment
8: Quality Products and Services

Strategy 53. Tell your team what their total compensation is really worth. If you are a growing company and can't afford to compete on salary alone—compensate your team in other ways. Offer flextime, additional vacation days, telecommuting options, doggie daycare, extra maternity or family leave, chocolate chip cookie breaks, summer hours, employee discounts … you get the picture! Anything you can do to help your team achieve more life balance will be appreciated and can be monetized to help you be far more competitive than many larger companies. It's often the little things that help you attract and retain top talent!
This strategy builds:

1: Commitment, Enthusiasm & Respect
2: Fair Compensation
7: Delighted Employees
9: Long-term Thinking

Strategy 54. Communicate high standards. Tell your team about your organization's accomplishments, breakthroughs and what distinguishes your company from the rest of the pack. Tie news to your cultural and financial goals and provide regular progress reports to employees as well as your suppliers, community and customers. It's not enough that your managers and executives know about the successes and accomplishments. Strong relationships are built on open communication and lifting up those around you, so they can be more than they dreamed they could be. Everyone wants to be on a winning team—let your employees know they are on one!

This strategy builds:

1: Commitment, Enthusiasm & Respect
5: High Standards
9: Long-term Thinking

Strategy 55. No surprises. Be certain everyone knows your *Perfect Workplace* attributes, your vision and what each person needs to do to create a better workplace. Use every means at your disposal to communicate repeatedly what's in it for me (WIIFM). Show your team how their contributions impact them personally as well as the company and your customers. Get managers engaged—every employee should know what's expected of them as your organization evolves.

This strategy builds:

2: Fair Compensation
5: High Standards
10: A Highly Skilled Team

Strategy 56. Coach leaders to *Smile*. This may seem too simple, but smiling creates positive changes in your workplace for two reasons. 1. Smiling and laughing release naturally occurring chemicals in our bodies that uplift moods and 2. Smiling is contagious. Leaders at every level in your organization set the mood in your workplace. Leaders are role models and their behavior significantly impacts your business performance. Try walking around with a frown and see what type of reaction you get from others. Now try smiling—it works!

This strategy builds:

1: Commitment, Enthusiasm & Respect
3: Coaching to Lead and Inspire
7: Delighted Employees
10: A Highly Skilled Team

Strategy 57. Examine your physical work environment from a fresh perspective. Take a tour of your facility with the specific intent of looking at it as if you were seeing it for the first time. Look at the images posted on your walls and bulletin boards. Are the images generally positive or negative? What about the outside of your facility? Is it clean and inviting or littered and depressing? Are the bathrooms clean? Is the break room and meeting spaces bright and cheerful? These things say a lot about your company and the expectations of its leaders. Walk around and examine the surroundings and ask—Does what I see make me feel good to be here? Would I want to work for this company if I knew nothing else about the business? If the answer is no in any area, recruit some people to help you design a more pleasing environment.

This strategy builds:

1: Commitment, Enthusiasm & Respect
5: High Standards
6: Team Empowerment
7: Delighted Employees
8: Quality Products and Services

Strategy 58. Examine your company communication and newsletter. Is the tone positive? Does it inspire? Do the words serve you well? Imagine the difference in outcomes between "We are at war with our competition" versus "We create innovative services and products that delight our customers." The first option is aggressive and places employee focus on your competitor and the second option is positive and fosters employee ideas that build rather than destroy. Words have power, so choose them wisely.

This strategy builds:

1: Commitment, Enthusiasm & Respect

3: Coaching to Lead and Inspire
7: Delighted Employees

Strategy 59. Rent a DVD or CD of Martin Luther King's "I Have a Dream" speech. Share it with your managers and leaders. Listen and see the images painted by Dr. King's inspiring words. Creating a "vision or picture" of the future is very powerful. It is impossible to listen to this brilliant orator without being moved on a very deep and emotional level. Do your messages inspire? Infuse your communication with language and emotions that enliven, enthuse, and build trust, hope and commitment. Words paint pictures in your mind's eye. When your desired outcome requires your team to move beyond there current thinking, take the time to create a masterpiece!

This strategy builds:

1: Commitment, Enthusiasm & Respect
3: Coaching to Lead and Inspire
5: High Standards
6: Team Empowerment
7: Delighted Employees
9: Long-term Thinking
10: A Highly Skilled Team

Strategy 60. Use a pocket notebook to record everything you see people doing right. Give a pocket notebook to each manager and tell them to make a note every time they see someone doing something that supports your *Perfect Workplace* vision and behaviors. Now recognize those actions with a thank you note, a great job comment, a recognition certificate, a "caught in the act" employee highlight on your intranet site or bulletin board, in the performance appraisal or with a smile. The key is to provide simple tools to help your leaders shift their thinking to look for and expect positive behaviors. It's a simple but powerful truth—we truly do attract what we project and expect!

This strategy builds:

1: Commitment, Enthusiasm & Respect
2: Fair Compensation
3: Coaching to Lead and Inspire
4: Superior Customer Focus
7: Delighted Employees
8: Quality Products and Services

Strategy 61. Customize recognition and rewards so they are meaningful to the recipient. You can find out a lot about someone by looking at their work space. Do they have a cat or a dog? Do they have young children? Would they value time off? Do they like movies? What type of books do they like to read? What's their favorite restaurant or store? Do they love electronic gadgets? Do they collect stamps? Taking the time to customize a reward that recognizes outstanding performance communicates that you value the recipient as an individual. A small personalized award is far more meaningful than a "one size fits all" big ticket item.

This strategy builds:

1: Commitment, Enthusiasm & Respect
2: Fair Compensation
7: Delighted Employees

Strategy 62. Post *the positives* on a bulletin board. Highlight positive customer comments, employee testimonials about helpful teammates, thank you notes for great customer service, outstanding team quality achievements, or community service awards that your organization has received. Positive actions create more positive actions. It raises the bar and makes people feel good about where they work!

This strategy builds:

1: Commitment, Enthusiasm & Respect
3: Coaching to Lead and Inspire
4: Superior Customer Focus
5: High Standards
6: Team Empowerment

7: Delighted Employees
8: Quality Products and Services
9: Long-term Thinking
10: A Highly Skilled Team

Strategy 63. Let your team members plan the celebrations. This strategy helps spread the workload for coordinating special events. It also helps build a sense of community and enables new ideas that keep your celebrations fresh and exciting. When you share the responsibility for planning celebrations, they become more meaningful because people have a hand in how they turn out. Share the fun!

This strategy builds:

1: Commitment, Enthusiasm & Respect
6: Team Empowerment
7: Delighted Employees
10: A Highly Skilled Team

Strategy 64. Provide tools that help coworkers recognize each other's contributions. Print note cards that say "I heard about your great work" or "I wanted to thank you for …." Leave a blank space for people to fill in the rest. Distribute these cards so everyone has an opportunity to write a personalized note to commend a coworker for a great job, or a habit that supports the *Perfect Workplace* goals.

This strategy builds:

1: Commitment, Enthusiasm & Respect
5: High Standards
6: Team Empowerment
7: Delighted Employees

Prioritize Strategies to Achieve Your Goals

Now that you've selected your strategies, it's time to prioritize them. Review the *Guideline for Choosing Your Best Strategy* to confirm that you've selected a balanced set of strategies that map to your needs and goals.

Is there a strategy that you could easily implement that would quickly address a need and a goal? If so, this is low hanging fruit—start here. Start with the simple things that will help you maximize your return on your time and cost to implement.

What is your biggest pain? This is your largest void or gap between where your organization is now and your vision of a *Perfect Workplace*. These are your biggest problem areas. You will want to choose more strategies to address this area.

If you'd like more help prioritizing your strategies, use the *Prioritizing Your Strategies* template that follows. It's not necessary to complete the template, but it may be helpful if you are struggling with where to start first.

Prioritizing Your Strategies Template Instructions

☑ Use the *Strategy Description* column to write down ten to fifteen strategies you've selected as possible actions you will take to fix problem areas and achieve your *Perfect Workplace* goals.

☑ In the ***Meets Survey Needs*** Column, assign a number to each potential strategy. Use only one number per strategy. Assign the number that most closely reflects the level of urgency for each strategy.

1—Meets a Critical Need (Very large gap between your current state and your *Perfect Workplace*)

2—Meets an Important Need (Large gap between your current state and your *Perfect Workplace*.)

3—Meets a need (Small gap between your current state and your *Perfect Workplace*)

☑ In the **Maps to Vision & Goals** Column assign a number to each potential strategy. Use only one number per strategy. Assign the number that most closely reflects the level of importance given your *Perfect Workplace* vision and goals.

1—Very Important
2—Important
3—Somewhat Important

☑ In the **Impacts Key Habits** Column—simply list all behavior numbers the strategy builds. For example, if you select strategy 48 from the *Perfect Workplace Strategy* table—it strengthens these key top performing workplace behaviors—1,5,6,7,8,10. Write down those numbers in the template column for that strategy.

☑ In the **Does it Stretch Your Team and is it Reasonable** Column— simply answer *Yes* or *No*.

If no—can the strategy be adapted easily so it is reasonable? Can you stretch it if needed to inspire a meaningful improvement? If not, take it off the list for now. You can revisit this strategy as your organization evolves.

Prioritizing Template

#	Strategy Description	Meets Survey Needs	Maps to Vision & Goals	Impacts Key Habits?	Does it Stretch Your Team? Is it Reasonable?	Total *(Add points in shaded columns.)*
1						
2						
3						
4						
5						
6						
7						
8						
9						
10						
11						
12						
13						
14						
15						

After Completing the Template:

1. Add the points in the shaded column and write the score for each strategy in the "Total" column. For example, if you chose strategy # 51(*Form a pay-plan committee.*) and rated "Meets Survey Needs" with a **1** (*Meets a Critical Need),* and a **2** (*Important*) in the "Maps to Vision & Goals" column—you would add 1 + 2 and place a **3** in the total column.

2. Do you have a YES in the "Does it Stretch Your Team and is it Reasonable?" column? If not, see if you can adapt your strategy easily so it is reasonable or does stretch your team. If not, take it off the list for now. You can revisit this strategy at a later date.

3. Now prioritize based on your points. The *lower* the score, the *more critical* your need and *the more important* it is to your *Perfect Workplace* vision and goals.

4. Now check to see that you've balanced your efforts across all of the key habits. In the "Impacts Key Habits?" column,

verify that you have addressed every key area—1 through 10 somewhere in the strategies that you've prioritized. Each category (1-10) represents a key behavior needed to create a *Perfect Workplace*. If you're missing one, see if you can adapt one of your strategies to address the missing category or select a different strategy that helps you fill in the missing gap.

Overcome the 9 Barriers to Change

Organizational changes, even when positive, can fall short of expectations. But, there are steps you can take to help your organization maximize the benefits of the strategies you've just selected.

To stay on track, you need to plan for possible issues. You can do this by being aware of the change barriers, so you can build steps into your plan that keep potential issues from limiting your business teams' success.

In a 1988 survey, top executives were asked what inhibited the success of their efforts to grow and improve. The barriers they identified are listed here in order of importance. The first one listed is the most important to success, two is the second most important and so on. [5] I've also listed the strategies here that help you minimize potential obstacles, so you can achieve your goals faster.

1. **Lack of reinforcement on the job**

- □ Do you have a plan to support the behaviors needed in a *Perfect Workplace* through training, and regular recognition and rewards at *all levels?*

- □ Do your compensation and performance systems help people in your business stay focused on what's important?

- □ See strategies 2, 3,5 and 10 to address this possible issue.

2. **Interference from immediate work environment**

- ☐ Are your managers ensuring their teams have the tools and resources they need to do their job well? One of the fundamental responsibilities of a manager or supervisor is to make certain their team has what they need to succeed.

- ☐ This means manager need to be walking around, talking to their team (strategy # 18)

- ☐ Are people relying too much on email? (strategy # 43)

- ☐ Are managers learning new skills so they continuously improve their effectiveness? (strategy # 44), and ...

- ☐ Are leaders empowering their teams to help them identify the best solutions? (strategy # 28).

3. **Non-supportive organizational culture**

- ☐ Do you provide opportunities for your team to form meaningful bonds, and to satisfy our fundamental need to socialize? (See strategies 7, 8, 15, 17, 19, 20, 29, 35, 48 for possible strategies)

- ☐ Do your team members have a means to influence and contribute to your organization's success in meaningful ways? (See strategies 2, 3,4, 5, 6, 12, 14)

- ☐ Are your managers well trained and compensated based on their *cultural* and *financial* achievements? (See solutions 24, 25, 26, 45, 46, 52)

4. **Perception of impractical training programs**

- ☐ Do you provide effective training programs? (See strategies 1, 2, 3, 16, 46)

- ☐ Do you provide ongoing on-the-job training, mentoring, and coaching in addition to the initial orientation? (See strategies 4, 5, 6, 7, 27, 48)

- ☐ Do you use tools such as recommended reading, low-cost online learning programs, and instructor lead training that address needs specific to your workplace? (See strategies 9, 17, 32, 44)

5. **Perception of irrelevant content or changes**

- ☐ Do your S.P.I.R.I.T. strategies map to the gaps between your vision, goals and current workplace behaviors?

- ☐ Did you use your *Perfect Workplace* vision and goals and survey results to confirm that the strategies are relevant?

- ☐ See "Guidelines for Choosing Your Best Strategies" in this chapter.

6. **Discomfort with change and associated effort**

It is uncomfortable when we step out of our comfort zone. But we can counter this by communicating and inspiring people.

- ☐ How are you preparing your team for change? Are you including them in creating the solution? (See "Imagine Your *Perfect Workplace*" brainstorming exercises).

- ☐ Does your team understand both the personal and company benefits of strengthening your workplace? (See strategies 1, 8, 11, 17, 22, 23, 25,29, 30, 32, 33,34, 36, 39, 40, 41)

Everyone wins when they step out of their comfort zones. That's how our comfort zone expands, it is how we grow. Feel the fear and do it anyway—that's the definition of courage!

7. **Separation from inspiration or support**

- ☐ Connect and Communicate, Communicate, Communicate! Use everything at your disposal to keep the vision, objectives and goals in front of people.

- ☐ Does everyone in your team know *why* you're making changes? Do they *understand* the vision and goals for a *Perfect Workplace*? (See strategies 7, 10, 11, 17, 18, 22, 23, 55)

- ☐ Have you told your entire workforce how they can contribute? Do they know the perfect employee contributions—*the new standards?* (Use Your "Top 10 *Perfect Workplace* Employee Contribution List" you created in the *Imagine* step. Also see strategies 7, 17, 22, 23, 24)

- ☐ Your vision and goals were designed to inspire, so use them. Tie them to your employee orientation process. Reward behaviors that support the *Perfect Workplace* vision and goals. Publish your visions and goals on your web site, company intranet, and on your bulletin boards.

- ☐ Coach your managers and executives to communicate and walk the talk. Your leader's actions must be congruent with your *Perfect Workplace* vision and goals. (See strategies 33, 41, 42, 43, 44, 45, 46, 52)

8. **Perception of poorly designed/delivered programs**
   Notice the keyword is *perception*.

- ☐ Do you give your staff members a voice in the design of your solutions? (See strategies 1, 2, 3, 5, 6, 14, 17, 28, 30, 31, 33, 35, 43, 48, 52)

- ☐ Get feedback through suggestions, ideas, and use committees to help build joint ownership. You'll gain valuable insights so you can make effective changes. By broadening participation, your staff will be far less likely to perceive your program as poorly designed because they have a hand in developing the solution.

9. Pressure from peers to resist changes

- ☐ *Remember your informal leaders you identified in the Survey step?* Engage them as active participants, and you will minimize this potential barrier. Their influence helps you build positive support for transforming your organization into a top performing team.

- ☐ Use open two-way communication (See strategies 1, 7, 8, 16, 17, 22, 23, 32, 41, 42, 54)
- ☐ Manage by walking round (See strategy 18)
- ☐ Ask for suggestions (see strategies 2, 3, 10, 14, 28),
- ☐ Recognize and reward habits that build a better workplace (See strategies 6, 25, 26, 29, 39, 40, 55)

Use these strategies to create positive energy and to prevent negativity from derailing your goals for a *Perfect Workplace*.

You may have some people in your workplace that are stuck in negative thinking. But, eventually these folks will convert or will need to find an environment that will support their negativity. They will no longer fit into your positive culture as your workplace gets stronger.

If you have someone who is especially disruptive, then you'll need to work within your established polices to constructively resolve the unsupportive behavior or get the right people on the bus. You need to proactively address behavior that negatively impacts the health of your organization. Negative behavior destroys morale.

Update Your Plan

Now take the strategies that will help you reach your goals and put them on your project schedule or checklist. Assign resources and dates for completion. It's important to get your strategies on paper with target completion dates. You will accomplish *10 times more* and in less time, if you commit your strategies to a measurable plan.

Adjust your target dates as you review dependencies (*what needs to happen first*) and resource availability.

As you update your plan, you will develop realistic expectations for the time required to implement your *Perfect Workplace* and *Top Performing Team strategies*. You will gain more clarity about what strategies you can do concurrently, and which ones may have to come later.

Remember, early wins build confidence and positive energy. They create momentum and make subsequent changes easier.

Your plan is your roadmap. It will help you stay on track. However, sometimes you may need to make adjustments based on changes in your organization. When that happens, simply update your plan by changing resources, adding or editing tasks, adjusting the scope of work, or changing target completion dates.

4 Guidelines for Changing Plan Completion Dates

As you progress, you will inevitably have to make decisions about extending target completion dates. Business conditions and resource changes can impact your schedule and delay the benefits you want to achieve. Consider these four guidelines to help you stay on track.

1. Understand the need for the change. Can you do anything to keep your desired benefits on track? Add a resource? Reprioritize another task?

2. Ensure you are moving forward and making progress, even if it's in small steps.

3. Verify that you and your team are focusing your energies on those areas that provide the biggest return on invested time.

4. Stay true to your objectives and goals; don't sacrifice the change benefits for speed.

Staying on Track

If you find you're routinely missing your target dates, find out why.

- □ *Do you have the right person assigned to the slipping tasks?*
- □ *Does your team have the necessary skills and tools?*
- □ *If not, can they acquire the skills or tools in a timely manner?*
- □ *What can you (or someone else) do to help you and your team succeed?*
- □ *Can you can add resources or outsource some of the work to stay on track?*
- □ *Can you break your strategies into smaller pieces, so you can start seeing benefits sooner?*
- □ *Can you simplify your strategies and still get the same or similar benefits?*
- □ *Is it possible that you were overly optimistic about what you could accomplish in the time you estimated?* This is not uncommon when you're passionate about the outcomes.

If you've:

- □ Verified you have the right resources assigned and they have the tools they need to succeed
- □ Examined the possibility of outsourcing or adding resources
- □ Divided your strategies into small pieces and simplified them as much as possible without sacrificing your desired outcomes …

Then it's likely that, in your zeal, you created target dates that don't give you a realistic amount of time to accomplish your goals.

That's okay; zeal and enthusiasm are great qualities! They will help you inspire your team and achieve the extraordinary. Examine what you've accomplished so far. How long did it take you and your team to complete what you've done up to this point? Consider the exercises that you completed in previous steps. Take that information and revise the amount of time you think you'll need based on your history and team's abilities.

Make the necessary changes to your plan. Review your prioritized strategy list to double check that your plan maps to your priorities and biggest needs.

More Resources

Here are some additional resources that can help you and your team create a better workplace.

Books

- ☐ *301 Great Management Ideas from America's Most Innovative Small Companies* Edited by Leslie Brokaw

- ☐ *301 Ways to Have Fun At Work* by Dave Hemsath & Leslie Yerkes

- ☐ *1001 Ways to Energize Employees* by Bob Nelson

- ☐ *Ask And You Will Succeed: 1001 Ordinary Questions to Create Extraordinary Results* by Ken D. Foster

- ☐ *Fish! A Remarkable Way to Boost Morale and Improve Results* by Stephen C. Lundin, Ph. D., Harry Paul, and John Christensen

- ☐ *Business Communication* Harvard Business Essentials and the HBS Press

- ☐ *Good To Great: Why Some Companies make the Leap…and Others Don't* by Jim Collins

- ☐ *First, Break All the Rules* by Marcus Buckingham and Curt Coffman

- ☐ *Influence: The Psychology of Persuasion* by Robert B. Cialdini, Ph. D.
- ☐ *Managing To Have Fun by* Matt Weinstein
- ☐ *Make Their Day!: Employee Recognition That Works* by Cindy Ventrice
- ☐ *The 1001 Rewards & Recognition Fieldbook* by Bob Nelson, Ph.D. and Dean Sptizer. Ph. D
- ☐ *The Power of Thinking Big* by John C. Maxwell
- ☐ *Transfer of Training: Action Packed Strategies to Ensure High Payoff from Training Investments* by Mary L. Broad and John W. Newstrom
- ☐ *What Would Buddha Do at Work? 101 Answers to Workplace Dilemmas* by Franz Metcalf and BJ Gallagher Hateley

Online[6]

- ☐ For more tools, strategies and templates see http://motivation-at-work.com. Don't forget to check the client access page! Your username is team and your password is spirit. Please use all lower case letters.
- ☐ For inspirational posters, artwork, accessories, employee awards and trophies see http://www.successories.com.
- ☐ For affordable items to help you inspire and motivate see www.baudville.com
- ☐ Creative Gifts Galore for gift baskets to recognize and reward employees go to http://creativegiftsgalore.net
- ☐ The incentive shop for electronics and higher-end reward programs can be found at http://www.theincentiveshopinc.com.
- ☐ For summaries of the latest management and leadership books go to http://www.executive-book-summaries.com. This is an effective and affordable leadership development tool.
- ☐ Harvard Business Online for articles, reports and resources to help your business grow go to http://www.hbsp.harvard.edu.

- □ Association for workplace learning (ASTD—American Society of Training and Development) see http://www.astd.org/ASTD
- □ Society for Human Resource Management http://www.shrm.org/
- □ For discounted books with free shipping go to www.amazon.com
- □ *Top 10 Reward, Recognition, Award, and Thank You Ideas go to* http://humanresources.about.com/cs/compensation/tp/recognition.htm

Next Steps

Congratulations you know have a detailed plan designed specifically for your organization! In this chapter, you discovered the guidelines for choosing your best strategies. Refer back to these as you continue to make improvements in your company.

You have over sixty strategies and ideas you can use to create the business of your dreams, and get everyone moving in the same direction.

You understand the priorities and steps you need to take to fill in the gaps between where you are now and where to want to go.

You also have specific strategies to overcome potential barriers and you know the steps you need to take to set realistic completion dates.

You have methods to help you minimize delays and distractions. You have a compass to help you remain focused and a list of over twenty-five additional resources you can reference for more help and support.

Now it's time to build leaders who can help you transform your organization into an extraordinary business. No employee motivation plan would be complete if it didn't address the *most important driver* for a successful transformation—your managers.

Chapter 7 | Step 5:Inspire Your Managers

"The deepest urge in human nature is the desire to feel important."

~ John Dewey

I begin this chapter with this wonderful quote by John Dewey[7] because it is at the foundation of what motivates people. We humans have a deep desire to feel important and to belong to a bigger community. Your workplace certainly qualifies as a community.

The desire to feel important and to belong is very powerful. If you let this thought guide you in your business everyday, you'll naturally make decisions that are aligned with creating an energetic, positive environment and a *Top Performing Business*.

In this chapter you will learn how to inspire and development top performing leaders. You'll discover:

- ☐ How your managers impact your workplace and bottom line
- ☐ The 7 reasons why people leave or become disengaged
- ☐ Why inspiring your managers before you develop them is so important
- ☐ The 10 Traits of Top Performing Managers
- ☐ The difference between managing and leading, and why it's important to understand the difference
- ☐ To beware of the "Management Trap"

- □ The 8 Enlightened Leader Behaviors
- □ Over 90 different strategies, tools, and resources to help you develop the leaders around you
- □ The 10 Actions that build manager/employee trust
- □ How listening impacts your business, and where to download a free assessment you can use to help your managers improve their listening skills
- □ 5 Strategies to Super Charge Your Performance Standards
- □ 18 ways to help your leaders refine and strengthen their communication skills
- □ 17 simple strategies that show respect in the workplace
- □ Which comes first, improving your culture or getting the right people on the bus
- □ 15 other resources you can use to help you inspire and develop your managers

Now it's time to build leaders who can help you transform your organization and take your business to the next level.

Manager Impact

A word of warning. People are not motivated by rewards and recognition alone. If it were that easy, every business would be filled with happy, enthusiastic, and committed employees. Rewarding performance and behaviors that are aligned with your goals is an important component of any workplace development program. However, this approach will not stand alone.

You can waste a lot of time, energy, and money giving away "prizes" to motivate your employees with very little impact. To transform your organization into a *Top Performing Business*, your leaders' behaviors must be in step with your *Perfect Workplace Vision* and *Goals.*

The best reward and recognition program in the world cannot offset the negative impact of leadership behavior that is inconsistent with what you want to accomplish.

Extraordinary workplaces create top results! Your leaders (this includes managers, supervisors, and executives at every level) must *walk the talk* if you want to transform your organization into an extraordinary business.

Imagine the impact to your organization if you implemented a program to recognize employees who provide exceptional customer service. At the same time, your managers don't take the time to greet your customers, and they don't give your employees the tools they need to provide outstanding service. Does that seem ridiculous? Yet it happens every day in many companies.

Your managers have the greatest influence on your employees and their ability to do their job well. They have more impact than your policies, procedures, incentive programs, and executive leadership combined. Is your employee turnover acceptable? Have you lost top performing employees? Do you have people on your team that were once very productive, but now lack commitment and enthusiasm? If so, you'll want to understand why people typically pull away from their workplace.

The 7 Reasons People Leave or Disengage

People leave a company or *become disengaged* because:[8]

1. The job or workplace is not as expected. (This is often tied to ineffective management behaviors.)
2. The job is not a good fit for the person's strengths or preferences.
3. They don't receive enough coaching and feedback.
4. There are too few growth and advancement opportunities.
5. They feel devalued and unrecognized.
6. They are stressed from work/life imbalance.
7. They no longer trust or have confidence in their leaders.

As you examine the top reasons for employee turnover and employee disengagement, it's easy to see why managers have so much influence over employee performance. Individual managers have significant control over the quality of a person's workplace experience, and ultimately a team member's quality of life.

Managers and the Workplace Experience

Let's look at some of the manager actions that impact the quality of your workplace.

- ☐ Are your managers generally upbeat and friendly or are they stressed out and closed off? A manager's mood and behaviors sets the tone for his/her department. It really does run down hill!

- ☐ Do your managers convey a sense of urgency to remove barriers and provide the tools their team needs to do their job well? This communicates how much you really care about the quality of your employees' work.

- ☐ Managers usually make the hiring decisions. Do your managers know how to ask the right questions to determine good job fit? Do they screen for qualities that support a healthy organization? Are they rushing the hiring process using the "find a warm body" approach? If so, you will see the impact in your workplace and on the bottom line.

- ☐ Do your managers recognize people for doing their job well? Do they provide immediate and constructive feedback to help their team build important skills?

- ☐ Do your managers actively engage employees in decisions to empower their team? This practice helps people feel valued and can provide superb insights and ideas to help your business grow dramatically.

- ☐ Do your managers ask their team how to improve procedures and policies? Do they know the career goals of their direct reports? Do they coach employees to help them develop the skills needed to advance or move into other areas of interest?

- ☐ Do your managers DWTSTWD (Do What They Say They Will Do)? This is critical for building credibility and trust.

- □ Are your managers open to feedback and suggestions? Do they act on suggestions and recognize those individuals who bring solutions to the table?

- □ Do your managers allow sufficient time for their team to recharge their batteries? Balance is critical for maintaining top performance. People without balance eventually burn out. Leaders will de-motivate if they relentlessly push for more, without providing recognition and the crucial breathing room needed for recharging. Employees start to disengage when they think that no matter how hard they work, it's "never enough."

These are just a few of the many ways that managers influence the employee workplace experience. It's critical that all leaders are connected directly with the transformation process. They need to be actively engaged, and just like employees, need to feel valued and important. Get your managers involved in defining the leadership development process.

Why Inspire

Disengaged managers create disengaged teams. Inspire managers by helping them see how much influence they have. Mid and entry level managers need to be reminded regularly about their critical role in shaping the quality of your workplace and bottom line. It's very easy for managers at these levels to become disengaged if they feel disconnected from top executives and feel undervalued.

This chapter is titled "Inspire Your Managers" for a reason. I could have used "Develop Your Managers," but that does not paint a complete picture.

Inspire means to energize, to spark, to engage, and activate. *See the difference?* If you want enthusiastic, energetic employees—inspire your managers first, then develop them.

Inspire managers by engaging them in the transformation process. Use the information you are learning here to teach them about their pivotal role in your organization. Align them with the *Perfect*

Workplace vision and goals. Help your managers understand how their actions personally impact the lives of your employees, as well as your bottom line. Being a manager is a *very important position in a company*, but it is often grossly underappreciated.

Inspire managers by filling them with a sense of purpose. To inspire also means to motivate. Inspired and well trained managers create *Top Performing Teams*.

Managers get disengaged when they do not feel they are part of the big picture, and when they do not grasp and appreciate how much influence they have. There's no magic switch that gets flipped when an employee is promoted to a supervisory position. They require coaching and training now more than ever. They also need to feel valued.

The T*op Performing Workplace Habits* apply to each and every level in your organization, especially your managers, because they directly influence your cultural and financial results.

The 10 Top Performing Workplace Habits

1. Display commitment, enthusiasm, and respect
2. Compensate fairly for "contributions"
3. Use coaching practices, not supervising
4. Focus on superior customer service
5. Have high work standards
6. Empower team members to have a voice in decisions
7. Have a strong sense of community and team spirit
8. Continuously improve the quality of products and services
9. Support long-term growth in actions and words

10. Are inspired, well-trained and dedicated to continuously improving their skills

Thank your managers for their contributions. Give them the tools and the training they need to do their jobs well. By creating this SPARK, you'll create momentum that will begin to resonate throughout your business. That's why you INSPIRE—then develop.

Managers and Leaders

We've talked about why your managers are the single most influential motivator in your organization. However, we can't develop great managers without also addressing great leadership practices. There is often confusion about the terms *leader* and *manager*, their roles, and which people in your organization are leaders versus managers. So, let's look at that before we go any further.

The basic difference between *leading* and *managing* is that management is about *process* and leadership is about *purpose*. Most business owners, executives, and managers need a mix of leadership and management skills. That doesn't mean that managers never lead and leaders never manage.

Leaders inspire a group to come together for a common goal. They motivate and coach people to keep them connected and eager to move forward. They set a direction, communicate it to everyone and keep people energized when the going gets tough. They focus primarily on *purpose.*

Managers figure out *how* things will get done. They create the systems, build the teams, and create the plans, operating procedures, and incentive programs etc., so an organization can accomplish its goals. So the focus is primarily on *process*.

Beware of the Management Trap

The traditional definition of *management* taught in many institutions of higher learning is that management is about the business, not the people. So, people are only important as a way of getting the job done. *Ouch!*

Are you starting to see the problem with the definition of *management* and how most organizations view leaders and managers?

Managers are often seen as leaders in waiting. The "leaders" are the senior executive strategists inspiring their team to succeed. The problem is the title *manager* has become synonymous with the people who only *manage the process or the business*.

This type of thinking strips away the importance of the critical leadership skills managers need to develop in order to create top performing workplaces and businesses.

It is never just about the process—it is about the people who perform the processes! Managers cannot effectively manage a process or system that requires people to operate, if they can't effectively lead the people who control the process.

Leadership skills are needed throughout the organization—not just as the officer and senior executive level.

Resist the temptation to segment leadership and management skills by position. If managers, executives, and business owners have people reporting to them, they need a combination of management and leadership skills. However, the focus will vary by position.

The Difference in Focus

Marcus Buckingham and Curt Coffman explain the difference in positional focus very well in *First Break All the Rules*. To paraphrase, the more senior the position, the more the leader tends to look *outward*. Senior leaders tend to focus primarily on the future, at alternate routes, at market trends, business development, joint venture opportunities, and shareholder relations. The focus tends to be more long-term in nature and outside the organization.

Managers generally look *inward*. They are looking inside the company. Their focus is on their team's strengths and weaknesses and how to best get everyone working together to accomplish the organization's goals and objectives. They are more focused on the short term, but good managers know they need to make tactical decisions that are aligned with the company's long-term interests. They need to be great coaches.

The primary activities are simply different. Personal style will vary, but most business executives and owners have a mix of both management and leadership skills. Both skill sets are necessary to run a successful business.

Great care should be taken when building leadership teams to ensure you have balanced skills and complimentary strengths on your team. Leadership skills provide the direction, while management skills provide the systems that allow a company to grow.

In all leadership positions though, whether manager, supervisor, owner or senior executive, leadership skills need to be in the mix. Management cannot just be about process.

The 8 Enlightened Leader Behaviors

There are eight common characteristics of managers and executives who lead top performing teams. These are the leadership behaviors that drive the organizations that are in the top 20% in their industry, company, or market.

I call these the *Enlightened Leader* behaviors that build *Top Performing Teams.* Enlightened Leaders are business owners, managers, supervisors and executives who regularly practice these behaviors.

They are very simple, yet very powerful and can be learned. All you need are *inspired* leaders that are committed to their ongoing development.

<u>Enlightened Leaders:</u>

1. Are good coaches

2. Value input from their team
3. Are trusted
4. Listen well
5. Set and communicate high standards
6. Are good communicators
7. Walk the talk (DWTSTWD—Do What They Say They Will Do)
8. Treat others with respect

These leadership behaviors create a highly engaged, positive, super-motivated, and high achievement workforce. These behaviors were broken down to their simplest form for clarity. They are observable and easily measured.

These actions, if practiced consistently, will have a profound impact on your organization. The *Enlightened Leadership* behaviors support the *Perfect Workplace* categories you used during the survey step. Each tool you used or developed in each step is designed to work together with the next step. So, you accomplish positive changes in your workplace faster.

The 10-category approach (Survey I) in the Survey chapter was designed to help you assess employee beliefs, evaluate your gaps in leadership and management skills, and measure the impact of the strategies you implement. As you conduct follow up surveys, you will be able to measure your progress. Just ask for the division where each respondent works as outlined in the survey. That allows you to measure your growth by comparing survey rating trends with your financial and cultural changes. You'll also be able to quickly see which areas require attention and which are flourishing.

Integrate the *Enlightened Leadership* behaviors into your management screening, hiring, evaluation, succession planning, and training and development processes. This will help you select and develop *Top Performing Managers who* create *Top Performing Teams.* Of course, these qualities are in addition to the other skills, process or industry knowledge you require for specific job responsibilities.

Let's review the *Enlightened Leadership Behaviors* one at a time.

Good Coaches

In some organizations, coaching has taken on a negative meaning as it has become synonymous with counseling for underperformance. Coaching is not a negative.

A coach prepares his or her team by instructing, advising, influencing, and grooming. They find and strengthen the appropriate skills needed to build a complete team. Great coaching is positive, proactive, consistent, and constructive.

Think of the greatest sports teams—the Super Bowl Winners, the Olympic Gold Medalists, the World Series Champions. They got there because they had great coaches. So too, top business leaders have great coaches.

Great coaching raises performance levels by helping employees understand what they need to do and how they can best do it. Good coaches provide the game plan. They motivate and encourage great work with regular feedback. They put teams together that have complimentary skills and actively develop their team's strengths. They address weaknesses constructively and make the most out of each team member's inherent abilities.

Great coaching is positive, proactive, consistent, and constructive!

Value Input

Do you recall the John Dewey quote? It's worth repeating again. *The deepest urge in human nature is the desire to feel important.*

There are many ways that leaders can encourage input. You can ask for it directly, meet with your team, facilitate brainstorming sessions or simply encourage your team members to come to your with suggestions.

However, they must be open to input and not criticize new ideas. Listen and reserve judgment. Often a suggestion that initially seems unworkable is the spark for a new approach that ends up saving an organization hundreds of thousands of dollars, or generating millions of dollars in new business.

Keep the input coming by giving credit to the people or person that contributed. Say thank you, celebrate, and reward active participation. If the input isn't feasible, that's okay. Sometimes the timing isn't right or there is a better or more cost-effective approach. Follow up and thank *everyone* who volunteers input, regardless of whether the idea is implemented.

Receive the stuff that's hard to hear with gratitude. This may seem strange, but coach your managers to take a deep breath when they have a strong reaction to an employee suggestion or comment. Give it time to sink in. Are they reacting to the delivery? Most often the suggestions that are hardest for us to hear are the greatest opportunities for growth. Encourage candid feedback and then ask your team for recommended solutions.

Are Trusted and 10 Behaviors that Build Trust

How do you build trust between my managers and employees? It's simple. What behaviors help you determine whether you trust someone?

1. Trust comes when you get to know someone. When you feel like they are interested in YOU.

2. Trust and leadership are about relationships. You can't trust someone you don't know. Good managers create opportunities to interact and connect with their team.

3. You trust people who aren't out to win at your expense. You trust people who use win-win strategies.

4. You trust people who appreciate your contributions and give credit where it's due.

5. You trust people who realize that growth and innovation bring risks. People who inspire trust forgive a mistake and help resolve setbacks.

6. You trust people who do what they say they will do (DWTSTWD).
7. You trust people who are direct and constructive. You trust people who confront negative behaviors that hurt them or the team.

8. You trust people who value you by listening to your concerns and ideas.

9. You trust people who communicate respectfully. They don't talk down to you or belittle you.

10. Trust comes to those that admit when they make a mistake and aren't afraid to apologize when appropriate.

Listen Well

People cannot feel valued if they don't feel heard.

Great leaders are almost always great listeners. When you listen well, you tell the speaker that you value them and their input.

Good listening skills help you keep your finger on the pulse of your organization. You become more receptive, so you can act before potential issues become major barriers. Focused listening helps you make better decisions and adjust course quickly when needed.

When leaders don't listen well, costly mistakes can occur that could otherwise be avoided. If you are a fast processor and are "thinking ahead," you risk missing a critical insight, drawing the wrong conclusion, or missing a better, faster way to accomplish something.

Listening well keeps your organization moving in the direction you want. You can make a big difference in your results and in the quality of your professional and personal relationships if you change your awareness and are willing to practice a few simple listening techniques

For more information about listening and to download a free listening assessment, go to the tools and services chapter of http://www.motivation-at-work.com. Feel free to pass the assessment around to your managers. Most people are surprised when they do a quick self-evaluation. On average, people listen with only 25% efficiency and then only retain a fraction of what they do hear. It is a skill worth developing.

Set High Standards and 5 Supercharging Strategies

Teams don't get to the Olympics or the World Series without high standards. In the business world, high standards mean—impeccable quality measures, top-tier customer service, team members that are enthusiastic and committed. It means your team members show up on time ready to contribute, and they don't pass off problems for the next guy to handle.

In addition to the obvious benefits of high standards, they are also critical to recruiting and retaining top talent. The reality; if your standards are just average, your top performers will leave, and you'll have difficulty recruiting the best candidates.

People want to be on a winning team. If you want to build pride in your workplace—set high standards.

5 Strategies to Supercharge Your Performance Standards

1. Support high standards with clear communication and good coaching.

2. Provide the tools your team needs to accomplish your new standards. Remove any barriers.

3. Make certain standards are realistic, given where you are now. Use the Crawl, Walk, Run approach. Stretch and condition your team first with small steps to build momentum and to get them ready for higher levels of performance.

4. To get new standards to stick, align your reward and recognition programs, performance management, and selection systems to support your changes.

5. Give people time to celebrate and recharge their batteries. If you don't make time for fun, continuous improvement can backfire in the form of employee burnout. Watch closely for signs of stress. Break your changes into small pieces.

   This may seem a little overwhelming, but it is achievable—one step at a time. **Every breakthrough starts with a single step!**

Are Good Communicators

Here are 18 strategies to help you refine and strengthen their communication skills.

1. Simply start with the words you choose. Positive words create powerful results!
2. Tell your team about what's working well. Don't focus solely on the areas that need improvement.

3. Provide valuable information. As you craft your team messages, ask *how can I contribute or help?*

4. Ask employees questions, and express sincere interest in both work and non-work related events when talking to your team.

5. Help others laugh. This releases chemicals in our brains that make us feel good. Of course humor should be appropriate for the workplace. It should build people up, and never tear someone down.

6. Show faith and trust in your team. Provide guidelines; be clear about what you want to accomplish; but resist the temptation to micromanage.

7. Say hello as you pass people you work with and smile!

8. Congratulate team members who do something that supports your goals and *Perfect Workplace* vision.

9. Say *thank you* to show your team you appreciate their contributions.

10. Always share good news as soon as possible!

11. Choose vivid words that paint a picture of your vision. Choose to inspire, build up, and energize.

12. Celebrate successes and cheer for your team.

13. Give words of comfort when needed.

14. Never allow negativity to hinder progress. Help mend relationships as soon as possible.

15. Teach, don't just tell.

16. Praise people for a job well done.

17. Get out of the office to talk to people face to face. This is missing in many companies.

18. Acknowledge people for their contributions and share the credit for success. No one becomes a champion alone.

Walk the Talk

This is also known as DWTSTWD—Do What They Say They Will Do. You've heard the saying *actions speak louder than words.* Well, that is more important for leaders than anyone else. We expect more from our leaders. Managers and leaders at all levels are expected to set an example. Respect is earned on both sides of the employee—manager relationship.

When managers don't follow up, act in ways that are incongruent with the best interests of the company, or use different standards for their own behavior than for their employees, you lose credibility.

A manager is in a critical position. He or she directly impacts your bottom line, the quality of your workplace and the lives of the people who report to them. If they are not trustworthy, and if they lack integrity, they simply should not be in a leadership position. The opportunity for significant damage to your organization is far too great. Consult a legal professional with expertise in employment law, but promptly address any issues associated with ethics, integrity, or trustworthiness.

Treat Others with Respect and 17 Respectful Strategies

Respect may seem like a no-brainer, but as of this writing, there were over 12,000 books written about how to treat people well in the workplace.

Most people are not intentionally disrespectful. Sometimes our actions or the words we choose are simply misinterpreted. They are not received in the manner we intended. Choose your words with great care.

We humans are notorious for creating mountains out of mole hills. Often, conflict in the workplace is simply a result of incorrectly interpreting a statement or action. Instead of asking for clarification, the "offended" individual mulls over the event in their mind until it becomes so big that it impacts their performance and their relationship with the "offending" individual. Meanwhile, the "perceived guilty party" has no idea what happened or why the other person now treats them differently.

The best approach is to be attentive to behaviors that change abruptly. For example, if you have a team member who always smiles and greets you every morning and then suddenly stops, find out why. Don't make assumptions, ask, "*Is everything okay*?" It may not have anything to do with you or work, but it could also be something that could easily be cleared up by simply asking a question.

Let's take a look at 17 simple strategies that show respect in the work place.

1. Listen attentively.

2. Ask for opinions and input.

3. Thank people for their efforts.

4. Be considerate in your words and actions.

5. Recognize people for their contributions.

6. Place decision-making authority at the appropriate levels.

7. Empower employees with well-written guidelines, and not policies that treat them like children.

8. Treat people with dignity.

9. Craft messages that build self-esteem especially when you counsel someone.

10. Provide opportunities for team members to connect with employees in other departments and with company managers and leaders.

11. Choose your words carefully. They can lift people up or tear them down. It is your choice.

12. Pay attention to your team, you can't get where you want to go without them.

13. Honor your team by doing what you say you will do.

14. Show simple courtesy. Ask your employees—How are you doing? How is your family? Open a door for someone. Offer to help carry packages. Little things really do mean a lot.

15. Don't be afraid to have fun at work. It's not a four-letter word. Research consistently shows that teams that laugh together enjoy working with one another and are top performers.

16. Respond quickly to employee questions.

17. Treat people how you would want to be treated if your positions were reversed.

Perfect Workplace Leadership Strategies

The following actions are from the list of strategies presented in *Reflect & Design* step. I've pulled out these strategies because they support the leadership development process. Choose those that best suit your unique needs. You'll probably choose several of these options based on your goals, resources needs and budget.

These strategies help your managers build top performing teams. Review them with your managers to get their input.

Don't' forget to see the *Other Resources* chapter that follows for additional training tools that can help your managers strengthen their leadership skills.

#4 **Provide opportunities for professional growth.** Growth doesn't always mean a pay raise or promotion. Learning opportunities help you develop future leaders. Managers should consider how they can develop their own skills while also providing opportunities for growth for their team.

#7 **Welcome your new hires with the red carpet treatment**. Get your managers involved directly in this practice. Ask managers about giving a welcome card to new hires signed by them and the rest of their team. Who introduces new team members? How much time do managers invest making new hires feel welcome? Are they ready with business cards, a clean workstation, your company goals, *Perfect Workplace* Vision & Employee Contributions?

#9 **Implement an *Enlightened Leader* development program.** You know the *Enlightened Leader Behaviors* now. Which managers in your organization would be good role models? Assign an experienced *Enlightened Leader* to new managers to act as a mentor. Use the ideas here or the recommended reading list at the end of this chapter for more help.

18 **Promote MBWA. M**anagement **By W**alking **A**round stimulates one-on-one communication. Set expectations that managers need plenty of floor time. Leaders get disconnected when they spend too much time in meetings and in their offices responding to email. Observe and reward your managers for building strong relationships with their teams.

#25 **Examine your employee performance review process**. Do you recognize and reward your managers and staff for contributing to *cultura*l AND *financial* growth? Be certain to reinforce your *Perfect Workplace Attributes* here. How do your managers want to be measured?

#26 **If it matters, measure it.** Hold your managers accountable for cultural and financial performance. Develop a simple *Balanced Perfect Workplace Performance Scorecard* and then use it for manager coaching, training, compensation, and performance evaluations. Consider trends by: total company, department, profit per employee, net profit, & performance for customer retention and referrals, as well as trends by manager for turnover, absenteeism, productivity, quality, and customer satisfaction ratings.

#33 **Empower your managers to recognize employee behaviors that build great customer relationships with spot rewards.** Use scratch & win games as incentives. Employees scratch off the ticket to see what they win. Give away small monetary rewards, gift certificates, movie tickets, a free day off with a grand prize in the mix. Rewards don't have to be huge to be effective. Display winning employee photos in high-traffic areas. What other ideas do your managers have for developing stronger teams?

#39 **Confirm that your managers can and do explain how your compensation system works.**

#42 **Zap the "us *versus* them" thinking.** Provide opportunities for all team members to mix. Use company update meetings as an opportunity to network. Do departmental tours and have new hires and employees spend time in every department getting to know what they do. *Encourage your leaders to walk around and talk to people in various job functions on a regular basis.* Use your company newsletter or intranet site to highlight contributions from people in every department and functional role.

#44 **Challenge your managers and executives to learn a new leadership skill each month.** Set solid management selection criteria that are mapped to your *Perfect Workplace* goals and *Enlightened Leader Behaviors*. Then give your leaders tools and incentives to continuously improve.

#45 **Reward "enlightened leadership" behaviors.** Are you supporting your program by rewarding leadership habits that are tied to your *Perfect Workplace* goals? Every manager should review cultural and financial performance trends with their direct reports. Compare performance across departments so you know who is leading well and who might need help.

#46 **Use low-cost learning techniques.** Give away books, magazines or online email leadership development subscriptions to managers. Encourage them to learn and grow with your organization. See the "Other Resources" chapter for more ideas.

#55 **No surprises.** Be certain everyone knows your *Perfect Workplace* attributes and vision and what each person needs to contribute to create a better workplace. Use every means at your disposal to communicate repeatedly what's in it for them personally, and how individual actions impact the company and your customers. Get managers engaged—*every employee and manager should know how they are doing long before they get their performance appraisal.*

#56 **Coach leaders and managers to Smile**. This may seem overly simple, but smiling creates positive changes in your workplace for two reasons. 1. Smiling and laughing release naturally occurring chemicals in our bodies that uplift moods and 2. smiling is contagious. Try walking around with a frown and see what type of reaction you get from others. Now try smiling—it works!

60 **Use a pocket notebook to record everything you see people doing right.** Give a pocket notebook to each manager and tell them to make a note of the people and circumstances every time they see something that supports your *Perfect Workplace* vision and behaviors. Now recognize *Perfect Workplace* habits with thank you notes, certificates, a great job comment, note in performance appraisals etc.

Which is First, Culture or Leaders?

Many leadership books promote getting the "right people on the bus". That seems to be the latest buzz. So, I'm often asked—*What should come first? Should I get the right people on my team first or should I work on culture first?*

Here's what I tell my clients. In order for plants to grow, you need rich soil AND the right seeds. Your culture is the soil that nourishes the seeds which enables your business to grow. If you plant new seeds in bad soil, and without the right gardening tools, your seeds may not sprout. They will certainly not grow to their full potential.

So, you will need to fix your soil and get the right seeds. But, start first with your workplace, which is your soil, and get that moving in the right direction. You may also need to strengthen your current team with different skills. But, before you can select the right seeds, you'll need to know where you are now (surveys), and what you want your future workplace to look like (your *Perfect Workplace Vision* and *Goals*). Those steps help you identify the seeds you will need to grow into the beautiful garden you envision.

Next Steps

There are over 90 suggestions, ideas, strategies and tools to help you inspire and develop your managers presented in this chapter. Most of the suggestions and strategies are low or no cost options. They require time and commitment, but won't break your budget.

Keep your approach simple. Chose the strategies that fill your needs and help you reach your *Perfect Workplace* goals.

- ☐ Inspire your managers. Help them understand their critical role in the transformation process.

- ☐ Review your survey results. Where are your gaps in leadership skills?

- ☐ Give your leaders tools to succeed. Start with the *Enlightened Leader* Behaviors and then use the other strategies listed in this chapter as well as the valuable tools and resources listed under "Other Resources" at the end of this chapter.

- ☐ Consider using a leadership assessment so your managers can understand their own strengths, and where they can improve. There are several options listed in the "Other Resources" chapter.

- ☐ Examine your management hiring and succession planning practices. Does your selection criteria include a consistent process for determining good job fit based on the *Enlightened Leadership* Behaviors and your *Top 10 Perfect Workplace Habits*?

- ☐ Tie manager compensation to objective cultural measures in addition to financial performance. Track individual manager survey progress, turnover rates, absenteeism trends, and customer satisfaction. Get manager input about how they would like their performance measured, given your organization's transformation goals.

- ☐ Ask your managers to tell you about their biggest time wasters. You may discover that they spend a lot of their time on things that really don't matter. Find out what barriers need to be removed, so they can allocate time to the eight *Enlightened Leader* behaviors to support you in your transformation efforts.

- ☐ Now add your Leadership Development tasks with target completion dates on your project schedule or checklist.

Other Resources

Assessments

1. *Now Discover Your Strengths*, by Marcus Buckingham and Donald O. Clifton, PhD. This book includes a free online assessment. You will be given a unique ID and online login instructions within the book.

2. Look for the Kolbe-A™ index at http://kolbe.com. It will help you identify people who compliment your leadership team's strengths. You can take it online for US$49.95 (at print time).

3. Profiles International http://profilesinternational.com/ provides a wide range of assessment tools from background checks, to 360 Evaluations, to tools that measure job fit based on your organization's unique needs. They comply with all 13 of the U.S. Department of Labor Guidelines. Their price ranges are dependent on the tools you need and your volume, so you'll want to contact them directly for more information.

Books

1. ***Awaken The Giant Within: How to take immediate control of your mental, emotional, physical and financial destiny!*** *by Anthony Robbins. Published 1991 by Free Press, New York, NY.* Mr. Robbins merges inspiration and practical application better than anybody else. He is not afraid to put himself out there and openly shares his personal stories to help you connect with his message. He has the courage to walk his talk.

2. ***Positive Words Powerful Results*** by Hal Urban. Published 2004 by Fireside, New York, NY. This book can change your life. It's on my desk and I refer to it often.

3. ***The Power of Now: A Guide To Spiritual Enlightenment*** by Eckhart Tolle. Published 1997 by Namaste Publishing, Inc. and New World Library, 1999 Novato, CA. This wonderful book is one I recommend frequently. You can feel the energy jumping off the pages as you read it. Its message is simple, yet

profound and will help you and your leaders appreciate the intense power of being fully present.

4. ***Winning With People*** by John C. Maxwell. Published 1982 by Nelson Books, Nashville, TN. This book is all about relationships which in the end is what gets everyone working together, moving in the same direction and enjoying the journey!

5. ***The 7 Habits of Highly Effective People*** by Stephen R. Covey. Published 1990 by Fireside/Simon & Schuster New York, NY. There's a reason why this has been a best seller for so long. Change happens from the inside out and this great resource can show you how.

6. ***Good to Great (Why Some Companies Make the Leap…and Others Don't)*** by Jim Collins. Published 2001 by HarperCollins Publishers, New York, NY. This is a well researched guide for creating a business that will withstand the tests of time.

7. ***Encouraging the Heart: A Leaders Guide to Rewarding and Recognizing Others*** by James M. Kouzes and Barry Z. Posner. Published 2003 by Jossey-Bass, San Francisco, CA. This book helps you get to the very heart of enlightened leadership. It's filled with simple and effective ideas that can transform an environment into one of great meaning and peak performance.

8. ***The Daily Drucker: 366 Days of Insights and Motivation for Getting the Right Things Done*** by Peter F. Drucker and Joseph A. Maciariello. Published 2004 by HarperCollins Publishers, New York, NY. This is a great desk reference to help you when you're feeling stuck, or are looking for a new idea or approach.

9. ***Practice What You Preach: What Managers Must Do to Create a High Achievement Culture*** by David H. Maister. Published 2001 by Free Press/Simon & Shuster, New York, NY. This is a great empirical resource and wonderfully researched. I've recommended it frequently to support what enlightened

leaders have intuitively known and practiced for centuries. David Maister quantifies how behaviors can impact your business performance.

Leadership Training

There are many training options from free resources to moderately priced, and expensive, multi-day seminars. Use the crawl, walk, run method if you're just getting started, or if you need to work within a tight budget.

1. Refer to **www.motivation-at-work.com**. It's filled with powerful strategies and articles that help you build stronger workplaces and top performing teams.

2. For a daily dose of inspiration subscribe to ***The Daily Motivator*** by Ralph Marston at http://greatday.com. I am a subscriber myself and really look forward to the insights and wisdom Ralph shares in this six-day-per-week motivational tool. It's affordable, inspiring and will lift you up!

3. **www.briantracy.com.** Mr. Tracy has authored over 35 books and over 300 audio and video learning programs. There is a reason why he is one of the top management consultants and speakers in the world. To find ebooks, online learning programs, coaching, speaking programs and other great resources, check out the Brian Tracy International website. This is a great resource for leaders who want to build a top performing organization.

4. If you want to expand your consciousness and learn more about the **Science of Mind** principles that can help you be, do and create anything you want, see http://www.angelaperegoff.com. Angela Peregoff is an ordained Global Religious Science™ Minister and a treasured friend. Science of Mind is a philosophy and a way of life that can be applied to any religious affiliation you choose to practice. Check out her daily blessings for more insights, inspiration and genuine, universal wisdom to feed your soul.

5. The **American Management Associations (AMA)** is at http://www.amanet.org. They offer seminars and onsite training. American Management Association began in 1913 with the founding of the National Association of Corporation Schools. Their programs are priced higher than many other online programs and consulting firms. However, they are a resource with a long history and may be a resource you want to check out.

Magazines and Other Publications

1. *Motto* (formerly *Worthwhile*). This is not your typical leadership or management publication. It's a recent addition to business publications with a positive, uplifting focus on "Work with Purpose, Passion, and Profit". You can subscribe at http://www.whatsyourmotto.com/

2. The *Harvard Management Update.* It's a great source for summaries of various management and leadership topics. It also highlights research and findings associated with managing people. See http://harvardbusinessonline.hbsp.harvard.edu.

3. *Executive Book Summaries* at http://www.summary.com. This is a great place to start for monthly summaries of newly released business, management, and leadership books. You can also buy individual summaries to help you determine whether you want to read the entire book or incorporate it into your own leadership inspiration and development program.

Inspired and well trained managers create motivated employees and High Performance Workplaces. In this chapter, we covered a lot of ground. You discovered:

- □ Why your managers have the most influence on your workplace and bottom line

- □ The 7 reasons why people leave or become disengaged

- □ Why inspiring your managers before you develop them is so important

- ☐ The 10 Traits of Top Performing Managers
- ☐ The difference between managing and leading, and why it's important to understand the difference
- ☐ To beware of the "Management" trap
- ☐ The 8 Enlightened Leader Behaviors
- ☐ Over 90 different strategies, tools, and resources
- ☐ The 10 Actions that build manager/employee trust
- ☐ How listening impacts your business, and how to download a free assessment you can use to help your managers improve their listening skills
- ☐ 5 Strategies to Supercharge your performance standards
- ☐ 18 strategies to help your leaders refine and strengthen their communication skills
- ☐ 17 simple strategies that show respect in the workplace
- ☐ If you should start by improving your culture first or concentrate on getting the right people on the bus
- ☐ 15 other resources you can use to help you inspire and develop your managers

Now it's time to learn how to make changes that last. In the next chapter you'll learn how to *transform* your organization for the long haul. You'll discover how you can overcome the common obstacles that can keep you and your organization from reaching your full potential.

Chapter 8 | Step 6: Transform Your Organization

"Our past is not our potential."

~ Marilyn Ferguson

Your past results do not determine your future, unless you choose to do the same things you've always done. You now have the tools to transform your business into the type of workplace that creates the business results you want. You are only limited by your own beliefs. Tap into your *Perfect Workplace* Vision and Goals to keep your team inspired. Dare to dream big, and you will create amazing results!

Your surveys provide a snapshot of your team's beliefs as you begin and move forward. You have a detailed plan to help you stay on track and achieve results faster. Your team's vision of a *Perfect Workplace* and your SMART Goals enable top financial and cultural performance. You close the gaps between where you are now and where you want to go when you design your *Perfect Workplace Strategy.* You discovered the importance of inspiring and developing your managers. Now it's time for the sixth and final step—transforming your organization for ongoing growth.

If we are not growing, we are dying. Like growth, transformation is not a destination—it is a journey.

Call it continuous improvement, growth, or evolution. If we stay still, we become stagnant and die. So too, your organization must continuously strive to expand and grow in order to remain healthy. The process you discovered in this system is not a one-time only proposition. It is a proven way of doing business that enables an enthusiastic, dynamic, innovative, and healthy business community that withstands the test of time.

Growth and transformation does not necessarily mean you expand in size, sales volume, locations or the number of people you employee. It can mean that, if that is your vision and what your market wants.

To transform means you continuously evaluate and improve your performance as it relates to the needs of your market, your employees and shareholders. You keep the things that work well, and refine or remove the business practices that no longer serve you, your team, and your customers. You reinvent, adapt, evolve, and move forward. You become wiser because you are always learning and inviting your entire team into the process of ongoing transformation.

In this chapter we review the key actions you can take to make your changes stick. In change management lingo, this is called "institutionalizing your changes." When you make the Motivation-at-Work Six Step System part of your everyday operating practices, your business transforms into a top performing community filled with enthusiastic, innovative and committed people.

Your purpose in business is to give your *ideal customers* what they want, and then do that better than anyone else. When you align your people and processes with your purpose, you move into the elite business club. These are the highest achievers, the companies everyone admires, and the businesses in which people want to work.

In this chapter we'll review the highlights of the six-step process and the important relationship between our attitudes and results. You'll discover the critical factors for making your changes stick. You will learn how to stay on track by recognizing early warning signs that can limit your cultural and financial performance. You'll also get fifteen tips for diffusing negativity and change resistance.

Let's build momentum and positive energy around your business. If you want to grow, adopt beliefs and practices that support continuous review, refinement, and improvement. The Six-Step Motivation-at-Work System gives you the tools and strategies you need to build a *Top Performing Business* that is built to last.

Transformation in a Nutshell

It's worth highlighting the important relationships and fundamental principles in the six step system, so you gain absolute clarity about why and how this system works so well.

Beliefs and attitudes determine your company's financial performance. Keep at the top of your mind that our thoughts and beliefs literally create our reality. The surveys measure attitudes and beliefs about the things that determine your company's operating and financial performance. Their thoughts and beliefs drive your performance. So it's important to understand what your employees genuinely believe.

Employee attitudes don't just happen, they are a result. Leader and manager actions determine employee beliefs and attitudes. People don't start out unmotivated when they begin working with a company, they become that way. The good news is, you can change beliefs and attitudes by using the Motivation at Work strategies.

You get a "belief baseline" with your first survey. Then you continue to survey your employees to measure your progress, initially twice yearly. You can change to an annual schedule as your progress dictates.

You regularly update and refine your cultural plan to reflect your progress and evolving needs. You stay true to your *Perfect Workplace* Vision and Goals. This helps you accomplish your goals faster than would ever be possible if you proceeded without a plan.

You inspire and develop your managers because they have the biggest impact on your employee workplace experience. Their methods of managing and leading your team directly impact your bottom line.

Your leaders use the *Enlightened Leader Behaviors* to support your *Perfect Workplace* goals. *Perfect Workplaces* create *Top Performing Businesses*.

You make your changes stick by "institutionalizing" them. This means you provide a means to consistently measure progress. You measure what's important, and then create accountability in your performance management and rewards and recognition processes.

You get the right people on the bus by incorporating your *Perfect Workplace* Behaviors and Enlightened Leader Behaviors into your screening, placement and training processes.

You keep people engaged in continuous improvement, and encourage and reward active participation.

You communicate, communicate, and communicate your goals and objectives! Once is never enough! Develop a communication strategy that uses a variety of delivery methods and tools. Refer to the list of *Perfect Workplace Strategies* in chapter six for more ideas and tips.

You use or adapt the ideas presented in the list of *Perfect Workplace Strategies* to help you motivate, remove barriers, solve problems, and create positive changes in your workplace.

You continuously evaluate your results and adapt or refine your strategies to keep your business in top form.

Do something unexpected every once in a while, especially when you see a dip in your organization's energy level. You can expand energy by giving people something to smile about. Consider random acts of kindness like a day off to spend with families, a heart-felt thank you or a few hours at the ballpark on a warm sunny day.

Make It Stick and Measure What Matters

If something is important—it needs to be measured and monitored. To make change last, you'll need to integrate "cultural health metrics" into your ongoing financial reporting process. The surveys were designed to give you a simple way to measure your progress.

Here are some examples of traditional financial performance measures. The methods you employ to track your operating and financial progress depend on your business needs. Most businesses use more than a few of these methods to determine how they are doing.

- ☐ Sales trend comparisons from the same period last year
- ☐ Sales results compared to budget or forecast
- ☐ Net Profit or Loss Statements
- ☐ Trends in production and servicing costs (cost of goods sold/ produced)
- ☐ Gross and net margins by item, category, or department
- ☐ Trends in customer traffic or response rates to marketing efforts
- ☐ Productivity trends such as units produced per employee and/ or per hour or division
- ☐ Operating Expenses as a percentage of sales
- ☐ Quality Audits to track defects per units produced per team/ employee
- ☐ Product defective return rates
- ☐ Inventory turns to budget
- ☐ Return on Investment (ROI)
- ☐ Return on Assets (ROA)
- ☐ Return on Equity (ROE)
- ☐ P/E Ratio
- ☐ Debt to Equity Ratio
- ☐ Profit/Employee

The Missing Elements

These common measures miss a critical element; they do not include the cultural indicators that help you spot potential performance issues before they turn into negative financial or operating trends.

These traditional methods of measuring financial performance are absolutely necessary. However, they only provide a way to measure your performance after it has already occurred.

The health of your culture is a solid indicator of what will happen on your bottom line.

Employee beliefs and attitudes drive your financial performance. So, you need to measure and monitor the health of your culture with the same diligence you give to your financial performance. Think of it as "preventative medicine."

To make your changes stick—you must measure, monitor and hold your team accountable for making progress for both cultural and financial areas of growth. The beauty of this approach is that cultural improvements almost always indicate positive trends in financial performance. Exceptions to this rule are due to swift changes in your market demand or unforeseen circumstances such as soaring raw material costs or natural disasters.

The Four Vital Signs for Your Culture's Health

1. Employee Survey Trends
2. Absenteeism
3. Employee Turnover
4. Customer Satisfaction Ratings

If you set up a system to capture this information and then incorporate it into your regular business reviews, you will able to detect the early warning signs of employee disengagement and "de-motivation." This helps you proactively address issues before they become major barriers. Once issues are full blown barriers, they've taken root and are harder to resolve.

Cultural health issues show up on your financial reports in the form of negative trends in your sales, net profit, productivity, and quality. The key to success is to diligently monitor your cultural health, so you don't have to suffer consequences that can be prevented with early detection.

You enable early detection by regularly monitoring your cultural vital signs. Add the analysis of your "Cultural Vital Sign Reports" with our regular review of financial and operating reports. If your current business rhythms require you and your managers to review and address operating and financial reports every Monday, then that is also your day to review and address your Cultural Vital Signs.

Examine your business rhythms; these are the regular meetings and practices that evolve in organizations. Examples are reviewing sales reports ever Monday morning, making schedule changes mid-week based on traffic patterns, and weekly business operations meetings. Are your leaders examining and adjusting their actions based on their cultural and financial/operating performance measures?

The "Cultural Vitals" give you a balanced view of your business. This view provides you and your team with a holistic and natural way to build a top performing, healthy business environment.

As you monitor your "Cultural Vitals," you continue to reinforce positive changes and communicate the importance of your *Perfect Workplace Vision*. Company leaders can increase business benefits by embracing the power of Cultural Vitals. Ask direct reports for feedback about these reports every week, so they know managing cultural health is an important part of their job. Develop *Enlightened Leader* Manager Behaviors by asking your managers for specific strategies they will use to address any areas of underperformance.

Employee Survey Trends

Your survey is a Cultural Vital Sign and a valuable tool that allows you to measure your progress over time. You see positive or negative trends when you start comparing the shifts in beliefs with each subsequent survey.

Never forget the important relationship between our belief systems and our financial results. Surveys help you determine how you are doing, and which areas need attention.

You start with your baseline and then complete a new survey every six months until you reach your initial *Perfect Workplace* goals. Then you can move to an annual schedule if you are making steady progress. Continue to monitor the other cultural vitals in addition to your financial and operating performance trends. If you see negative trends, you may want to reassess your survey schedule.

The survey categories that measure and predict top financial performance are employee beliefs about your company's:

- ☐ Customer Service Orientation
- ☐ Empowerment
- ☐ Fair Compensation
- ☐ Quality of Products and Services
- ☐ Coaching
- ☐ High Standards
- ☐ Employee Satisfaction & Morale
- ☐ Commitment, Enthusiasm & Respect
- ☐ Long-Term Orientation
- ☐ Training and Development

When you complete subsequent surveys, you will look for positive or negative trends in these categories. You measure progress by comparing changes in the percentage of people who respond with Strongly Agree, Agree, Somewhat Agree, Somewhat Disagree, Disagree, or Strongly Disagree.

For example, let's look at a trend in beliefs around "Commitment, Enthusiasm and Respect" at a fictitious company.

Survey #	Strongly Agree	Agree	Somewhat Agree	Somewhat Disagree	Disagree	Strongly Disagree
1 Baseline	1%	8%	12%	45%	27%	7%
2 Baseline + 6 months	7%	29%	25%	19%	15%	5%
3 Baseline +12 months	23%	51%	19%	4%	2%	1%

In this example, there is clearly steady progress being made in how people view their workplace. In the baseline survey only 21% of the employees believe they worked in a *Committed, Enthusiastic and Respectful* business (indicated by strongly agree, agree and somewhat agree). Just twelve months later, with the third survey, 93% of the employees now believe they worked in a *committed, enthusiastic and respectful* organization. Can you imagine the difference in the energy level and performance results?

The impact of positive shifts in beliefs is very powerful. It is not uncommon for companies that actively apply the principles outlined here to see gains in net profit between 12% and 42% in as little as twelve to eighteen months. The critical driver for rapid improvement is senior leaders who are highly committed to the transformation effort.

Absenteeism Trends

Your attendance rate is one of the "vital signs" that measures the overall health of your organization. I'm not speaking of "physical health" here, but the motivation, energy, commitment, and engagement levels of your workforce.

If you are not measuring the trends in this area, I highly recommend that you start. I have been amazed by the valuable insights I've gained my reviewing absenteeism trends. You'll get maximum value by monitoring your companywide attendance rate in addition to tracking rates by division, department, and manager. This allows you to compare how individual managers or divisions are trending over time as well as how they stack up to your company average.

You may discover correlations between high absenteeism, productivity, quality, and absenteeism by manager. Generally, the higher the absenteeism rate, the bigger your challenges with motivation, productivity, and quality. Excessive absenteeism over time is an indicator of counterproductive managerial and leadership practices you'll want to address. Develop *Enlightened Leadership Behaviors* to create a top performing organization.

I once worked with a company that had significant productivity challenges in one of its divisions. After examining the trends, I discovered the division with the lowest productivity also had an excessive absenteeism rate. Furthermore, it was the *Manager* of the underperforming division who had the highest absenteeism rate. In a company of 1,200 employees, the manager of one of their largest divisions missed more work than anyone else in the entire company.

Unfortunately, that behavior had continued for years with no one addressing the issue because "he was so good at his job when he showed up." So over time, the division adapted a very causal attitude about deadlines, efficient operating practices, quality, and customer service.

With the changes introduced, and with the full support of the senior leaders, that same division had the highest quality and productivity rating in the company within 15 months. The past does not predict your future, but you have to be willing to make changes, even when they are difficult.

Employee Turnover

Like absenteeism, your voluntary employee turnover or retention rate is a "vital sign" that measures the overall health of your organization.

You'll get the maximum value by monitoring your companywide voluntary turnover rates in addition to tracking rates by division, department and manager. This also helps you see how individual managers or divisions are trending over time and how they perform in comparison to your company average.

Once you have the essential data, it is very simple to work your cultural health metrics into your performance management system. *A word of caution,* do not use any vital sign to determine a manager's performance rating or compensation if they had no ability to directly influence the outcome. This might seem obvious, but it is a common oversight when people have limited resources and time to adequately prepare for an optimal performance evaluation process.

For managers who are new to a position or area, jointly review the vital signs for the area as a *benchmark only*. Then any improvements they make during their tenure can be measured from that baseline. The important thing to remember is to get your managers involved in determining how they will be measured. Everyone needs to know and agree to the criteria up front, so there are no issues come review time.

I worked with a company after they lost their best manager because they missed this very important point. Imagine how you would feel if you were held accountable for something you had no control over. Always opt for fairness and be diligent about data integrity and getting agreement about how performance will be measured.

Customer Satisfaction Ratings

I place customer satisfaction with cultural vital signs because your customers' opinions are a direct reflection of your cultural health. It tells you how the people in your organization deliver customer value. If your team doesn't keep your customers happy, your customers will certainly look for a better alternative.

Employees throughout your organization need to see how they are doing in this area if you want to create a customer-focused culture. What you measure matters! That also means your employees need to know it's measured, and why and what they can do improve customer relationships.

Without customers, we simply have no business. Yet, customer satisfaction tools are often the most overlooked reports. Actions speak louder than words. If your team doesn't know what your customers feel, and if you don't discuss it relentlessly, your employees will naturally conclude that customer satisfaction is not a top priority. Share the positive and the not-so positive trends. Do this weekly and daily if you can.

12 Elements of Good Customer Performance Management

Do you have all the information you need to give your customers exactly what they want? If not, it's time for a tune up. Compare these twelve elements to your current system. Is there room for improvement? These processes don't have to be high tech, but a consistent approach that is easy to maintain will help you keep your customers coming back.

An effective customer performance management system:

1. Allows you to easily measure trends for what you do well, and what needs improvement. Reporting frequency should be weekly at minimum, preferably daily, and possibly hourly depending on your business model, sales volume, and number of locations.

2. Provides a *highly visible* way for your customers to easily provide feedback about their experience with your products, services, and employees.

3. Gives customers an opportunity to speak with you or a high ranking leader if they want to.

4. Provides prompt and effective responses to customer inquiries and comments.

5. Invites and encourages customer ideas, suggestions, and feedback.
6. Tells you what your customers value and want, so you can give it to them.

7. Allows you to communicate results to everyone in your organization and identifies required actions for delivering outstanding customer service.

8. Gives you specific actionable information that will help you improve your customers' experience.

9. Allows you to understand the lifetime value of your customer. *Who are your best customers?*

10. Helps you personalize service or product offerings so you can provide premium value to each customer.

11. Allows for easy, no-hassle returns for any item that doesn't perform as expected.

12. Is a key part of your performance management and compensation processes at every level in your organization.

Managing Change

The *Motivation-at-Work System* was designed to include all of the critical elements you need to make your potential continue to expand for years to come. If you follow the steps, adopt the strategies that best fit your organization, and use the tips provided to minimize obstacles, you'll be well on your way to achieving your *Perfect Workplace* and *Top Performing Business* goals.

However, as we've all witnessed first hand, even positive changes can encounter resistance. No change management discussion would be complete without reviewing the importance of senior level commitment.

Executive Sponsorship

If you want to create companywide changes, your senior managers must drive these changes. Global cultural changes need to be driven from the top down. Your senior leaders need to be ready to address behaviors within your leadership and management team that do not support a *Top Performing* organization. Even the best employee motivation program will not overcome the pitfalls created by incongruent leadership behavior.

This doesn't mean you'll be able to get everyone on board. But you'll want to convince at least 75% of your managers and leaders that the status quo is far more painful than the unknown.

Expect some resistance. There's a complex set of emotions that comes with any type of transformation, even if you believe the changes are generally positive. Your future is at stake. If you do not have the expertise you need on your leadership team, get help. Bring in a change expert to help you identify and resolve the potential pitfalls.

Ask your managers about their concerns with the changes, and then do what you can to answer their questions and remove barriers. Some people may feel threatened their influence will be diminished. Others may fear that you are adding more work with little or no payoff. Find out what you can do to address concerns as much as possible. Are there nonessential activities you can reduce for the time being? Do your managers fully understand the impact to them personally and to your company if you do not make the changes?

Perhaps your managers need to commit to extra duties in order for your company to reach its goals. If so, consider placing a time limit on additional responsibilities or limit nonessential duties. As you achieve your cultural and financial improvements, you'll be in a much better position to address issues of work balance.
As you progress through your *Perfect Workplace* plan, you'll create better processes that empower your entire team. When that happens, manager roles change to *coach* instead of *supervisor*. Make certain your managers understand how the *Perfect Workplace* changes help them too.

Find ways to include relationship building and socialization even when your team is very busy. People need to feel connected, especially during transitions. Build in time for networking. Consider working lunches with scheduled time for sharing ideas, concerns, and comments.

How do you quickly identify potential barriers to change? Use the Vital 4 to monitor your culture's health and progress.

These are the quantitative tools you can use to monitor your culture's vital signs. Start with your surveys; you already have those in place. By measuring and sharing trend data with your team, you support your financial and cultural objectives. You communicate the importance of these metrics by measuring them and then making people accountable for the progress in these areas, just as you do your financial performance.

Create Awareness

There are certain situations that occur in businesses, which can increase the likelihood of employee disengagement. By being aware of these circumstances, you can decrease the potential for steps backward. Situations such as managerial or organizational changes often are precursors of employee disengagement. This is especially true if a departing manager had a good relationship with his or her team.

Also be observant for a decline in interactions between your employees and customers. Observe closely to see if your team members and managers openly greet and attend to your customers.

Pay attention to employee body language. Does your team make eye contact; are they smiling and laughing? These are all signs of a healthy team.
Supplement your quantitative vital signs with good old walking around. Do this regularly, and ask your team for input and suggestions. Find out how they are doing, and if they need help removing any barriers. If you build relationships of trust, respect, and appreciation, you'll be able to address issues long before they become major problems.

Negativity and Individual Accountability

Two recent college graduates started working for a retail chain in their management training program. After several months of complaining to one another about nasty customers and unhappy employees, they decided to look for other work. But prior to quitting, they challenged one another to find at least one positive experience about working for this company.

They knew they were short term, so they weren't going to let "those people" get to them. So, no matter how someone spoke to them or treated them, they decided to respond with enthusiasm, courtesy and respect.

An amazing transformation occurred in their personal workplace experience. Soon after they started their experiment, customers didn't seem so nasty, and the employees actually seemed happy. People smiled at them, greeted them enthusiastically, and sought out and thanked them for their help. So did the workplace change, or did their change in attitude produce the positive reactions? The shift in their beliefs created an entirely different work experience.

If you can teach one thing to your employees that can make a profound difference in their work and personal life, it is the basic law of *like attracts like*. Another way to say it: we attract what we project.

So, the good news is that we can change our results if we change our beliefs and attitudes. Eternal pessimists will continue to attract the negativity they project. However, the positive folks will generate positive circumstances in their lives. Obviously there are business cultures that are more supportive than others. There are some that are toxic. However, you empower yourself when you take responsibility for creating your own reality. We become creators and are no longer victims.

15 Tips for Diffusing Negativity and Change Resistance

1. Relentlessly communicate the *Perfect Workplace* Vision, Goals, and Behaviors. When you engaged your team in the process of creating the vision, goals and strategies, you increased ownership across the organization. This strategy minimizes change resistance significantly, but it will not eliminate all pockets of negativity or resistance.

2. Share success stories early and publicly thank those who contributed to improvements. Remember, if you plan for early wins, you build momentum and diffuse negativity faster.

3. Seek to understand the cause of change resistance or negativity. Is it based on incorrect assumptions? Are different priorities, conflicting goals, or mixed signals creating frustration on your team? Did poor communication contribute to the situation?

4. Be ready to address legitimate concerns. Apologize if called for, but also teach your team that change is uncomfortable. Make certain they know that the alternative of doing nothing is far worse. Sometimes a reality check is needed.

5. Address negative behavior quickly. Communicate peacefully, and breathe normally to promote calm in difficult situations.

6. When addressing negative behavior, rephrase what you hear and observe. Avoid using "you" as it generates defensive responses. Rephrase with...This is what I think I heard…Is that correct?

7. Aim for win-win outcomes whenever possible. Your goal is not to overcome or force your views. Your goal is to change unsupportive behavior. You want the individual to understand how their actions hurt them and the workplace in which they work. Keep the end goal in mind.
8. Be ready for the eternal pessimists. They love to throw up roadblocks. When they do, repeat what you hear and then ask the person for constructive suggestions for resolving the problem. You may get a blank stare, but it also takes the

wind out of their sail and encourages them to rethink their position.

9. Ask a pessimist to substantiate a negative comment. Chances are they won't be able to back it up. If they can, listen attentively and acknowledge their comments. Set expectations that comments are to be constructive.

10. Always state your position clearly and positively.

11. Remember that obsessive pessimism is a sign of low self-esteem. See it for what it is, and don't take it personally.

12. Concentrate on facts, not character traits or issues that no longer matter. Get people inspired by what is possible.

13. Don't take things personally if someone doesn't want to get on the bus. You simply cannot allow the eternal naysayer to derail your transformation goals.

14. Some people are habitual pessimists and identify so strongly with their negativity that they simply will not change. You can't help them. Concentrate on creating positive momentum by working closely with those who support your goals. Limit the eternal naysayer's influence.

15. Follow your specific policies or procedures to get the right people on the bus. Use our *Perfect Workplace* attributes and behaviors going forward to help you identify people who are a perfect fit for your *Top Performing Business*.

Disruptive Behavior and the Eternal Pessimists

In a perfect world, everyone would enthusiastically embrace change. But, we know that's not how it works. So you may experience behavior that can undermine the goals for your organization's growth. *What if you have an employee who is a negative influence?*

The approach has to be taken in context with the bigger picture. To formulate the appropriate response, you'll need to consider the following factors.

- □ How does this individual's behavior differ from the general workplace given your survey results? If it's consistent with the behaviors of his/her teammates, a leadership issue may need to be addressed.

- □ Is the negative behavior out of character, or is it a long term pattern with this individual? If this person was once a productive member of your team and the behavior is recent, you'll want to determine the cause of the behavior change.

- □ Are there unusual circumstances contributing to this person's behavior? If this was once a productive, positive contributor, consider what you can do to help this individual improve.

- □ What are your policies and history for dealing with this type of situation? Proactively address negative behavior to clean up toxic cultures.

- □ Has this person's manager followed your formal procedures to effectively address the disruptive behavior? If not, why not?

- □ Is this individual wiling to change his/her behavior? Has his/her manager communicated clear expectations for improvement? Is the improvement strategy aligned with your policies and the *Perfect Workplace Behaviors*?

- □ What is this person's sphere of influence? If negative behavior is allowed to continue unchecked, it will poison your workplace. The higher the sphere of influence, the more potential for damage. Urgency is required to address unsupportive influences.

By all means, consult with a qualified human resources professional or employment attorney for guidance. Do what is best and fair for all concerned and you will position your entire team to discover their unlimited potential.

Moving Forward

The terms *Perfect Workplace* and *Top Performing Business* were used frequently as we moved though the six-step *Motivation-at-Work* transformation system. As we grow, we transform continuously improving the quality of our work and life experience. So transformation, like excellence, is a journey, not a destination. It is a philosophy, and way of living and doing business that helps us grow and expand personally and professionally.

As you and your team move forward on your journey together consider how far you've come. Take time now and then to appreciate what you and your organization have that's truly special. For if you push forward relentlessly and forget to enjoy the journey—you will miss the joy of creating something meaningful and extraordinary. Have fun and recharge often. Cultivating balance will help you avoid burnout, help you achieve more and you'll have a lot more fun along the way.

I laughingly call myself a *recovering Type A*. I spent a good part of my career working the 60 and 70 hour work weeks, frantically working to check the next thing off the list. I'd like to share something I've learned through my mistakes and missteps along the way.

So, here's a special note to "Type A" Leaders everywhere. It is okay to just BE every once in a while. We are human *beings*, not human *doings,* and are so much more than the sum of our accomplishments. If you can cultivate balance and inspire and empower others to do the same, you will have a much richer life and work experience than you could ever imagine.

Chapter 9: Dare to Soar

A Few Final Words

Helen Keller once said, "One can never consent to creep when one feels an impulse to soar."

My sincere hope is that you are inspired to pursue your goals and dreams for your organization with absolute passion. I hope that you feel the inspiration to soar because great accomplishments start with the actions of just one person. You make a difference!

Imagine what would happen . . . if we stopped thinking about work as just a way to earn a living?

Imagine what would happen . . . if everyone saw work as an essential ingredient of a fulfilling life?

Imagine a workplace filled with enthusiastic, committed and respectful people. Picture a workplace where people smile, laugh and work hard. They work together to help one another excel and share ideas eagerly. They are innovators. They are impeccably focused on the needs of their incredible customers. Together they accomplish remarkable results. This is a *Perfect Workplace and a Top Performing Business*.

Now is your time to be what you will. Your past does not predict your future unless you choose to continue to do the same things you've always done. Choose to soar!

Please share your success stories with us. Contact laura@motivation-at-work.com. Remember to check http://www.motivation-at-work.com for more tools, resources, and templates designed for *Top Performing Businesses*es and Enlightened Leaders.

Here's to you and your top performing team!

Laura Cardone

Chapter 10: Bonus Chapter

The Perfect Workplace Commitment

Perfect Workplace Commitment

I hereby decide to work by our organization's *Perfect Workplace* Attributions and Contributions. I choose words and deeds that build a strong work community.

Signed on the ________ day of ________ 2____

____

Your Signature

There's great power in making a declaration. When we make statements and commitments, we strengthen our resolve to take actions that are aligned with that declaration.

This certificate was designed to help you tap into the enormous energy created by a team's supportive declaration. Use the text provided here, or fine tune to fit your organization's specific goals or preferences. I've used similar team declarations in the past with great success. Use team declarations to inspire and empower. Help your employees and leaders understand how their words and deeds impact the quality of everyone's work experience.

Team declarations build commitment and enthusiasm, and pull people together in pursuit of a common purpose.

Help Us Spread the Word

We thank you for your purchase, and are grateful for your support. If this book resonated with you and helped you move closer to the desired outcomes you envision, please let us know. If you have a comment or suggestion that could help us make this system better; we want to hear from you.

Share your success stories with us and other like-minded leaders. Your insights, suggestions, and experiences can make a real difference in how our life at work evolves.

Help us spread the word. Share your thoughts with us and our subscribers, site visitors and customers. Send your insights, ideas, suggested resources and success stories to laura@motivation-at-work.com.

Success and Status Report Template

This template is designed to help you celebrate your successes and stay on track.

[Subject or Project Name] Period: ________ to ________

Project Manager: Project Team/Contributors:

Status Summary

[Summarize your progress. Indicate whether your tasks are on track as expected. Note major changes or discoveries.]

Completed This Period – Recent Successes!

[List achievements since your last status update. Provide supporting detail for changes to scheduled completion dates. Recognize special team member contributions!]

Schedule or Key Items to be Completed—Upcoming Period
[List key tasks or milestones that are in progress for the upcoming period.]

Item:	Target Date:	Person Leading:	Critical Date:*

* The date task should be completed to avoid delays.

Budget
[Summarize progress to budget if needed. If you want to request changes, describe the reason for the request.]

Issues to be Resolved
[List potential problems and their resolutions. Note how your team will stay focused on the vision and desired outcomes.]

Item:	Target Date:	Person Responsible:	Impact Date:*

*The date issue must be resolved to avoid delays to dependent tasks.

Goals for next review
[Highlight your most important activities that will move you toward your vision.]

Date of next success and status update: _______________

Wonderfully Enlightened Resources

You may find this to be a rather eclectic blend of resources, but that is also what makes it so valuable. This wonderful list of books and resources brings in the wisdom of multiple disciplines and perspectives. Taken together, they provide great insights and reveal what's truly possible when we know with our entire being, that we can do, be and create anything that we desire.

We are pure potential and unlimited possibilities. Explore this list, find what resonates with you and consider trying something that may not spark your interest at first glance. For in stepping out of our comfort zone, we expand our ability to conceptualize what's possible. In so doing, we grow and become more than what we were before.

Recommended Reading

Ask and You Will Succeed: 1001 Ordinary Questions to Create Extraordinary Results. **Ken D. Foster**. If you want to know how to get a different result, don't use the same thinking that created your current reality. This can be a life altering resource if used with deliberate intention. By simply asking different questions, you'll get different answers. Considering different perspectives provides you with greater clarity of purpose and opens new doors to limitless possibilities.

Awaken The Giant Within: How to take immediate control of your mental, emotional, physical and financial destiny! **Anthony Robbins.** Mr. Robbins merges inspiration and practical application like a master. He is not afraid to put himself out there and openly shares his personal stories to help you connect with his message. He has the courage to walk his talk. His insights and exercises can help you develop personal leadership skills that will serve you very well.

Encouraging the Heart: A Leaders Guide to Rewarding and Recognizing Others. **James M. Kouzes and Barry Z. Posner.** This book helps you get to the very heart of enlightened leadership. It's filled with simple and effective ideas that can transform an environment into one of great meaning and peak performance.

Fish! A Remarkable Way to Boost Morale and Improve Results. **Stephen C. Lundin, Ph. D., Harry Paul, and John Christensen**. If you prefer quick reads this may be a resource that will resonate with you. Don't mistake the size or format though for a less than powerful message.

Goals! How to Get Everything You Want-Faster Than You Ever Thought Possible. **Brian Tracy.** There is an art to designing the life and business you want. It requires more than what is taught in the typical goal setting seminars and books. This book guides you through a powerful process of creating compelling goals that are aligned with your unique values. It then gives you practical strategies to help you remove the obstacles that can limit your potential. Mr. Tracy has authored over 35 books and over 300 audio and video learning programs. There is a reason why he is one of the top management consultants and speakers in the world, so I encourage you to check out his other resources and tools at www.briantracy.com.

Good To Great: Why Some Companies make the Leap…and Others Don't. **Jim Collins.** Carefully researched, quantitative data that inspires. Mr. Collins and his team prove that you can, in fact, make a big difference in your organization in a very genuine and human way.

Influence: The Psychology of Persuasion. **Robert B. Cialdini, Ph. D.** This book is a must read for anyone one who wants to understand how the human psyche responds to circumstances, messages and environmental influences. This material is well researched and profound in scope. When we understand our underlying nature, we are able to make better decisions; free of both the deliberate and inadvertent attempts to influence our beliefs and actions. Only then can we be free to choose that which truly feeds our soul.

Make Their Day! Employee Recognition That Works. **Cindy Ventrice** This book cites dozens of real-life examples of recognition programs that work. You'll learn cost-effective strategies and how to integrate recognition into your daily routine

Positive Words Powerful Results. **Hal Urban.** Words have real power and we can use them to lift up or tear down. This book can literally change your business and your life. It's on my bookshelf and I recommend it often. This resource is a perfect training tool for leaders or administrators who want to create written or verbal messages that have positive impact. Words can inspire us and take us to places beyond what we think is possible. When you want to create something truly extraordinary, take the time to create a masterpiece. Mr. Urban shows you how.

Practice What You Preach: What Managers Must Do to Create a High Achievement Culture. **David H. Maister.** This is a great empirical resource and wonderfully researched. I've recommended it often to those who want to know more about the bottom line impact of building a top performing team.

She Wins, You Win. Gail Evans. Gail was CNN's first female executive vice president and is a *New York Times* bestselling author. In this landmark book, you'll learn the importance of being a team player and how to set up your own winning team. The common denominator that underlies long term business success is having a strong support network. Ms. Evans shows you how to build one.

The 7 Habits of Highly Effective People: Powerful Lessons in Personal Change. **Stephen R. Covey.** This is truly a classic and for good reason. Change happens from the inside out and this great resource can show you how to live the habits that build personal and professional effectiveness.

The Daily Drucker: 366 Days of Insights and Motivation for Getting the Right Things Done. **Peter F. Drucker and Joseph A. Maciariello.** This is a great desk reference for every business owner. It's filled with great insights, ideas and questions to help you discover new perspectives.

The Power of Now: A Guide To Spiritual Enlightenment. **Eckhart Tolle.** This wonderful book is one I recommend frequently. You can feel the energy jumping off the pages as you read. Its message is simple, yet profound. Let it guide you on your path of enlightened leadership, so you may know the intense power of being fully present.

The Project Manager's Desk Reference. **James P. Lewis**. Everything you wanted to know about project management, but were afraid to ask.

The Science of Mind: A Philosophy, A Faith, A Way of Life. **Ernest Holmes.** If you're looking for a personal foundation and a lifelong resource to help you discover your unlimited potential, this could be what you are looking for. Deeply spiritual, yet pragmatic, Mr. Holmes teaches and inspires us to consciously create the life we want by aligning ourselves with the universal laws of the universe.

What Would Buddha Do at Work? 101 Answers to Workplace Dilemmas. **Franz Metcalf and BJ Gallagher Hateley.** This work imparts wisdom as well as down-to-earth insights and strategies. This is truly a blend of spirit and practical matters at work. It's a resource you'll refer to often.

Transfer of Training: Action Packed Strategies to Ensure High Payoff from Training Investments. **Mary L. Broad and John W. Newstrom.** This resource gives you specific steps you can take to maximize the effectiveness of your training programs. There's power in training only if it leads to your desired outcomes. This book shows you how to design or select a program that works.

Winning With People. John C. Maxwell. This book is all about relationships, which in the end, is what gets everyone working together, moving in the same direction and enjoying the journey!

301 Great Management Ideas from America's Most Innovative Small Companies. Edited by **Leslie Brokaw.** This is a great reference to help you get unstuck. Just pull it out and open a page. You'll find a practical idea, insight or strategy that can help you build a better business.

301 Ways to Have Fun At Work. **Dave Hemsath & Leslie Yerkes.** Okay, I've said it before and I'll say it again. Fun is not a four letter word. Check it out, you might find something to lift the spirit in your workplace which translates to increased motivation, procitity, retention, profits… you get ht idea!

1001 Ways to Energize Employee. **Bob Nelson.** This is a great tool for expanding your pool of potential strategies. Based on the simple but uncommon approach of "you get what you reward", you'll get an almost endless stream of ideas to energize your team members.

Awesome Ezines, Magazines and Other Publications

1. For a **daily dose of inspiration and wisdom** subscribe to ***The Daily Motivator*** **by Ralph Marston** at http://greatday.com. I am a subscriber and highly recommend it. Mr. Marston openly shares his uplifting insights in this life-changing tool.

2. ***Motto*** **(formerly *Worthwhile*)**. This is not your typical leadership or management publication. It's a recent addition to business publications with a positive, uplifting focus on "Work with Purpose, Passion, and Profit". You can subscribe at www.whatsyourmotto.com.

3. **The *Harvard Management Update*.** It's a great resource for research summaries and findings impacting management and leadership. See www.harvardbusinessonline.hbsp.harvard.edu.

4. ***Executive Book Summaries*** at www.summary.com provides summaries of newly released business, management, and leadership books. You can buy individual summaries to see if you want to read the entire book or incorporate it into your own leadership inspiration and development program.

5. **Change your thinking and change your life** with the Science of Mind Magazine. See www.scienceofmind.com.

6. If you want to learn more about the universal principles that govern how we create our reality, see **www.angelaperegoff.com**. Angela Peregoff is an ordained Global Religious Science™ Minister and a treasured friend. Check out Angela's daily blessings for more insights, inspiration and genuine, universal wisdom to feed your soul.

7. To feed your spirit with **totally unique thoughts** see www.tut.com.

Cool Tools and Resources on the Web

1. **Brian Tracy International has hundreds of programs to help you achieve your goals faster.** See www.briantracy.com. You'll find tools and resources to help you with personal growth, time management, sales success and everything in between.

2. **For a simple, yet powerful approach for attracting more of your perfect customers.** See www.perfectcustomer.com. Their affordable tools will help you break past traditional marketing approaches that are ineffective and drain your energy and your budget. **Jan Stringer** teaches you how to attract more of your perfect customers while staying true to your unique values and strengths.

3. ***Are you serious about creating a top performing business?*** Then an effective coach is an essential component. You certainly wouldn't expect an athlete to make it to the Olympics or even a high school state tournament without a coach. The keys to choosing a successful program are finding the right fit and someone who walks their talk. Check out **John Assaraf** at www.onecoach.com. His firm helps entrepreneurs and small business owners increase their revenues and profits so they can live extraordinary lives.

4. **As a Motivation-at-Work customer, you get access to more strategies, time-saving tools, templates, resources and tips**. Just go to the *Client Access* page at www.motivation-at-work.com to login. Your user name is team and your password is spirit; all lower case.

5. **Get free tips and strategies for Enlightened Leaders delivered directly to your inbox.** You will get something that is truly special—ideas, thoughts and strategies that will lift you up, keep you on track, and raise your awareness ... so you can eliminate the obstacles and reconnect with purpose and passion at work. You will learn strategies to build peak performance with certainty and simplicity. Subscribe online at www.motivation-at-work.com. It's designed to be a quick read for busy leaders who also want to take their organization to the next level.

6. Go to **NOLO** at www.nolo.com for **legal and business tools** for small businesses.

7. For a **directory of business service providers** that includes everything from business cards to commercial real estate, see www.business.com.

8. See www.allbusiness.com for **articles and resources** to help you grow your business.

9. See www.surveymonkey.com to quickly and easily create **employee or customer surveys**. This tool is a low cost option and does not require a long term contract.

10. www.zoomerang.com is another option for developing **online surveys**. This option provides you with templates. To see more information about these tools see Chapter 3: *Survey*.

11. See www.surveysystem.com/sdesign.htm for more survey design tips.

12. O*NET, the **Occupational Information Network** provides detailed information about job duties for common occupations. Go to http://online.onetcenter.org.

13. See the **U.S. Department of Labor** at www.dol.gov for compliance information related to a wide variety of topics including: wages, disability, hiring practices and occupational safety information.

14. www.strengthsfinder.com is an **online assessment that helps you identify your top strengths**. You'll need to buy the book, *Now Discover Your Strengths*, by Marcus Buckingham and Donald O. Clifton, PhD to get a unique login ID. This is an affordable and effective way to help your leaders develop a better understanding of their individual strengths. The book is a great resource for managers who want to learn more about leveraging individual strengths and building a top performing team.

15. Look for the Kolbe-A™ index at www.kolbe.com. This is another **assessment tool** that helps you identify people with complimentary skills **for building balanced teams**.

16. Profiles International www.profilesinternational.com provides a **wide range of assessment tools from 360 Evaluations to tools that measure job fit based** on your organizations unique needs. They comply with all 13 of the U.S. Department of Labor Guidelines. Their prices are dependent on the tools you need and your volume, so you'll want to contact them directly for more information.

17. For **inspirational posters, artwork, accessories, employee awards and trophies** see www.successories.com.

18. For **affordable items that help you inspire**, motivate and thank your team - see www.baudville.com.

19. See Creative Gifts Galore for **gift baskets** to recognize and reward employees, honor customers, thank partners and celebrate special moments at www.creativegiftsgalore.net.

20. See **Lina Penalosa** at thewritesolutionllc.com for professional **copywriting solutions that are creative, unique and very effective.**

21. The **Senior Market** is a growing area of focus for many businesses and with good reason. For help with servicing this very important market, see **Sue Cunningham** at www.seniorresourcesgroup.com/speakingtopics.htm

22. To join an organization that propels women entrepreneurs into economic, social, and political spheres of power worldwide see the **National Association of Women Business Owners** at www.nawbo.org.

23. The association for workplace learning is ASTD (**American Society of Training and Development**) www.astd.org.

24. The Society for **Human Resource Management** can be reached at www.shrm.org.

25. To **find out how stuff works** see www.howstuffworks.com.

26. For the **best selection of books** on the planet, great prices and free shipping with most orders - go to www.amazon.com.

27. ***Top 10 Reward, Recognition, Award, and Thank You Ideas*** *www.*humanresources.about.com/cs/compensation/tp/recognition.htm.

28. The **Project Management Institute** www.pmi.org. This is a membership-based organization established in 1969. They provide training and certification, and represent project management professionals in a wide variety of industries.

29. The **American Management Associations (AMA)** www.amanet.org offers seminars and onsite training. They are a resource with a long history and may be a resource you want to investigate.

30. **If you can't find what you're looking for,** check out Google Answers www.answer.google.com/answers.

Notes and Bibliography

[i] *Customer Experience Report United States & Great Britain*. Research conducted by Harris Interactive® and sponsored by RightNow Technologies® in Q4 2005 in the United States (U.S.) and Great Britain.

[ii] Based on data from 20,000 interviews compiled by the Saratoga Institute. Reported in the *Harvard Business Review*, August 2005.

[iii] Bassi, Laurie J, Ludwig, Jens, McMurrer Daniel P. and Van Buren, Mark. *Profiting From Learning* Research White Paper by ASTD and Saba (2000).

[iv] McCormack, Mark H. *What They Still Don't Teach You at Harvard Business School* Bantam Books, Mark H. McCormack Enterprises, Inc. 1989

[v] Kotter, John P, *The Leadership Factor*. New York: Free Press, 1988

[vi] The links listed here were active at the time this program was developed. However, links and site content can change.

[vii] John Dewey (1859-1952) was an American philosopher and educator whose writings and teachings have had profound influences on education in the U.S. Dewey's philosophy of education, instrumentalism (also called pragmatism), and focused on learning-by-doing rather than rote learning and dogmatic instruction.

About the Author

Laura Cardone is President of Profits *with* Purpose Inc., a consulting and multimedia publishing company in Virginia Beach, VA. Laura has successfully led multimillion dollar companies and business divisions throughout her career. Her diverse background includes senior executive leadership positions in the technology, consulting, retail and publishing industries.

She is dedicated to providing tools and services that help business owners eliminate roadblocks so they can soar to new heights. Laura's philosophy is there are no limits to what you can be, do or create! She is dedicated to helping people build a successful business, meaningful work, and a balanced and fulfilling life. It is her sincere hope that you achieve your greatest personal and professional hopes, goals and dreams.

Laura and her husband Jim have three adult children Dawn, Patrick and John. They also have two very energetic golden retrievers, Chelsi and Sydney, who keep them busy walking and playing fetch.

Recent Awards and Distinctions:

- *Business Pioneer Award* from the National Association of Women Business Owners

- Certificate of Achievement from the *Center for Mindful Studies* in the Principles of Science of Mind

- CTM from Toastmasters International

- Board of Directors for the Southeastern Virginia chapter of NAWBO

- Recognized by the city of Virginia Beach for her commitment to improving the quality of local neighborhoods through community service in *The Neighborhood Leadership and Development Institute*

- *Chairman's Club Distinction for Outstanding Contributions* from Harris Connect

More Resources for You

Free Resource Page for Our Readers
This book contains templates, checklists, tools and links to online resources. As an added thank you, we've created a resource page specifically for our readers. Point your web browser to **www.motivation-at-work.com** and navigate to the **Client Access** page. Your username is team and your password is spirit, all lowercase. You'll get instant access to a *members-only resource page* that contains downloadable templates, tools and more.

Enlightened Leadership Onsite Seminar (3 Days)
This intensive program will transform your business and workplace forever. Business owners and managers will learn how to build an enthusiastic and highly motivated environment and eliminate the obstacles that limit potential. You'll reset your leadership "blueprint" so top performing financial success comes naturally. Plus you'll learn how to reduce firefighting, so you get to enjoy more of the journey!

Enlightened Leadership Teleclasses and Online Training
The principles of the *Enlightened Leader are* now available online. If you're interested in how you can achieve personal and professional mastery from the comfort of your own home or office, this program may be a great fit for you. Learn how to connect purpose, passion and extraordinary profits. For details, go to www.profitswithpurpose.com.

Life Directions
This online program helps you connect profits with purpose. You'll learn your personal mission and then create a plan to help you design a personal and professional life that maps to your unique definition of success. See www.profitswithpurpose.com for more information.

Speaking
Laura Cardone has a unique message that unites and inspires you to go beyond what you might think is possible. She merges the dreamer and the doer to illuminate while giving you practical strategies and tools to take your organization beyond the bottom line. To have Laura or one of our speakers appear live at your next event, e-mail info@profitswithpurpose.com or call 757-426-3554.